Personal
Recollections
of
Vincent
van Gogh

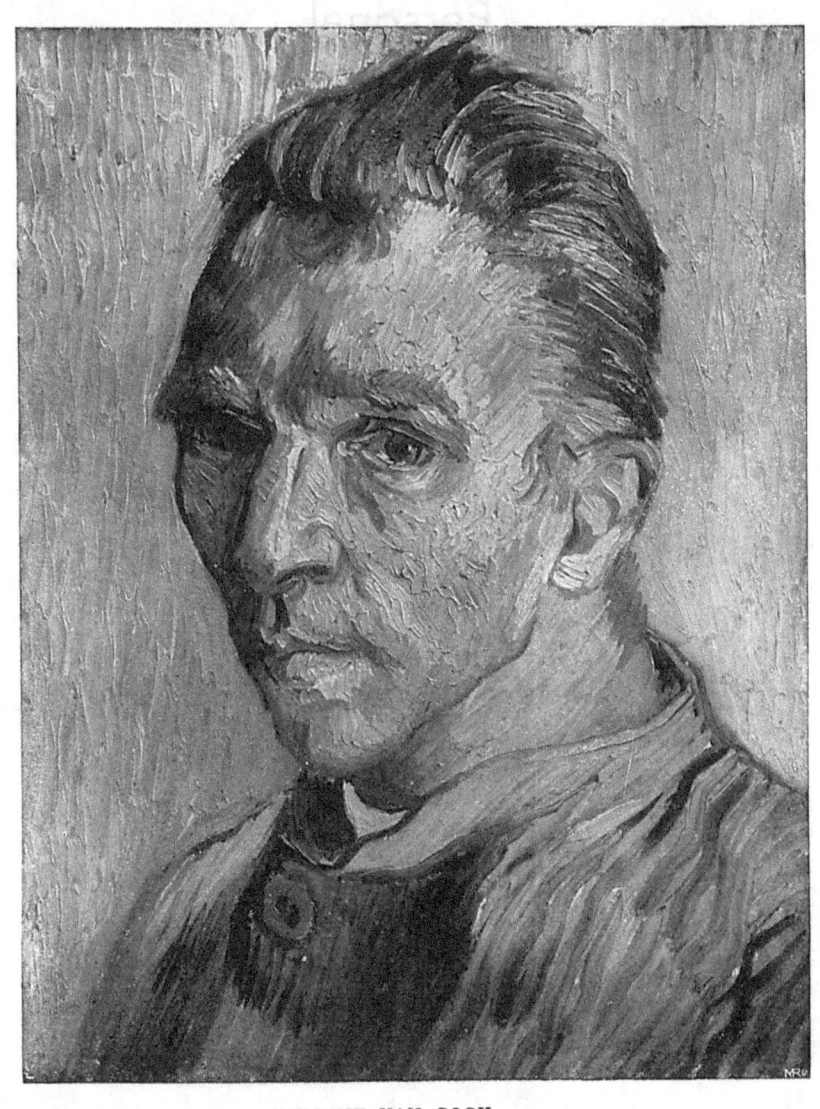

VINCENT VAN GOGH
painted by himself

Personal
Recollections
of

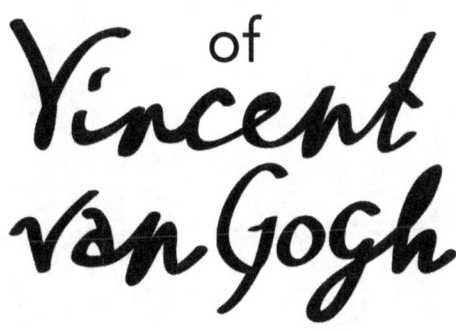

Elisabeth Duquesne Van Gogh

Translated by
Katherine S. Dreier

With a Foreword by Arthur B. Davies

Dover Publications, Inc.
Mineola, New York

Bibliographical Note

This Dover edition, first published in 2017, is an unabridged, corrected republication of the work originally published in 1913 by the Houghton Mifflin Company, Boston and New York.

Library of Congress Cataloging-in-Publication Data

Names: Gogh, Elisabeth du Quesne van, 1859-1936, author. | Dreier, Katherine Sophie, 1877–1952, translator.
Title: Personal recollections of Vincent van Gogh / Elisabeth Duquesne Van Gogh ; translated by Katharine S. Dreier.
Other titles: Vincent van Gogh. English
Description: Mineola, New York : Dover Publications, Inc., 2017.
Identifiers: LCCN 2016039351| ISBN 9780486809069 (paperback) | ISBN 0486809064
Subjects: LCSH: Gogh, Vincent van, 1853-1890. | Artists—Netherlands—Biography. | BISAC: ART / Individual Artists / Essays. | ART / Reference.
Classification: LCC N6953.G63 G64 2017 | DDC 759.9492—dc23 LC record available at https://lccn.loc.gov/2016039351

Manufactured in the United States by LSC Communications
80906401   2017
www.doverpublications.com

EEN der allerbelangrijksten, zeker de opmerkelijkste schilder uit het heden — in zijn waarachtigheid als kunstenaar, is de eerbiedwaardige, verhevenheid van Van Gogh.

W. STEENHOFF, *Groene Amsterdammer*.

Admirez-vous les uns les autres,
Admirez l'homme et admirez la terre,
Et vous vivrez ardents et clairs;
La vie est à monter et non pas à descendre,
Nous apportons, ivres du monde et de nous-mêmes,
Les cœurs d'hommes nouveaux, dans le vieil univers.

EMILE VERHAEREN.

There is no genius without a tincture of madness.

SENECA.

CONTENTS

ILLUSTRATIONS

FOREWORD

THE paintings of Van Gogh show soundness and lucidity of mind, in form and in color, and contain sure indications of generous human sympathies. All this combines to make an art work which is essentially aristocratic. His powerful stride leads us into the domain of cosmic unity, where the great artists cluster in Pleiades. Because so satisfyingly permanent they give that zest to life, showing that the ascendency of any human being, though handicapped by depressions and the sense of imminent misfortunes, will prevail over all those seemingly inherited material conditions.

It is blindness not to recognize in Van Gogh's paintings a fine balance of faculties, simplicity, and seriousness based upon a natural expression. He had no eye for compromise, for the devil of academic security of possession. He has ruled his domain with kingly power and made his visions beautiful, painting them in characters of rugged construction.

To see his master works is to realize his loyalty to his subjects, a singleness of purpose which is almost painful. His masterstroke is a prayer of thankfulness, his final thought a law of eternal energy.

As a seeker after some "new spirit," Van Gogh again verifies that, in avoiding conventional realism, art is vitally augmented change, suggesting so much, completing so little, yet conformable to the natural order of intuition and duration.

The ordinary person is not naturally delighted with a great break, as made by Cezanne, Van Gogh, Gauguin, Matisse, and Brancusi; with the determination not to go on imitating facts but to produce, instead, things of plastic, decorative beauty. Mankind nevertheless is always able to discern that sincerity is a necessity of occupation in an art work, and that there is a relation of the fact to the perfect idea, and to the perfect artist.

ARTHUR B. DAVIES.

INTRODUCTION

DURING the summer of 1912, Der Sonderbund of Cologne held an exhibition of modern paintings, representing especially those painters of various nations who are trying to express not only themselves but the spirit of to-day.

Europe is greatly in advance of us in this respect, ready to give a hearing to a group of earnest thinkers in whatever branch of thought, be it science or the arts. This is especially true of France, and that hospitable city, Paris, which is always ready to share all its knowledge and its thoughts with those who wish to enter its portals. Who has not heard of or met with those kind French dealers, men of moderate means, of plain birth, whose passion for art has made them true patrons, in the real sense of the word — men who have given assistance to young, struggling, and unknown painters or sculptors; who gave them their first chance by placing their work in their show-windows, or, by giving credit for material, offered them the first real opportunity for work; who, when asked by commercial friends whether the loss was not great, answered, as did Père Foinet, "No, for they always pay back unless death instead of fame first overtakes them"!

Germany, too, is trying to bring to life this spirit, in forming art associations throughout her large cities, which will enable artists to exhibit their work at almost no expense.

One of these new associations representing the modern movement is the Sonderbund of Cologne, which held an exhibition last year. From all over Europe people came to see and to learn. It was held in a large temporary structure, and of the twenty rooms, four were given over entirely to the works of Van Gogh. One hundred and twelve of his paintings had been gathered together from collections scattered throughout Europe. Here at last was an opportunity to study the works of a man who was deeply impressing and influencing artists and critics in many countries. They were not slavish followers, imitators, that one met, but men who were doing vigorous original work. Van Gogh seemed to have stimulated and opened out to them a whole new vision of color construction.

We reached Cologne after a long, dusty railroad journey and immediately drove out to the exhibition. The first room that one entered was the large hall with a single line of Van Gogh's paintings, all done in his last and most brilliant period, hung spaciously, so that each picture came to its full value.

It was like stepping out of a stuffy room into glorious, bracing air.

What courage and conviction had produced this vitality — these pictures vibrant with life!

How did Van Gogh secure this result?

The foundation of it all—his mind—what was it like, that made this extraordinary personality what it was?

That was the question that kept repeating itself, and I read all that I could find about him, in the hope of having it answered.

This simple, exquisite appreciation written by his sister seemed to me to give one more truly a keynote of understanding of his work than all the technical dissertations on his methods and achievements. Here, through his sister, one has the privilege of an intimate and sincere introduction into the life and work of the man. He had a broad education, a great capacity for work, a fine intellect, fed by incessant study, which, when concentrated upon art, developed both theory and practice. His knowledge of many languages opened out vast fields of literature on art and chemistry, and nothing which could be found relating to these subjects escaped him. The single-mindedness of his life alone made possible the progress which he achieved.

It was, however, also the philosophical problems of life that consumed him, and his tremendous concentration caused the tragic temporary mental breakdowns. For critics, therefore, to emphasize these periods of depression and insanity, as if the saneness were but a matter of lucid intervals, is about as unfair a proceeding as one can find. The conclusion of one critic, that Van Gogh was unable to "think straight" because of them, tempts one to ask the objector how many pictures by Van Gogh have been seen and studied, — not how many books or articles have been read?

The only criticism that can be made on the work of an artist is on his pictures, not on what he has written.

He is not a writer, but a painter. The medium chosen whereby to express the individuality—that is of primal value to the world. Therefore, by his paintings alone Van Gogh must be judged.

To any one who has made a study of color, Van Gogh's pictures will open a new door that leads to a future which the old masters never dreamt of. It is as revolutionary in painting as Giorgione's oil is to Botticelli's tempera-paintings — though oil is used by Van Gogh.

That he did not live to carry his work to completion, but must leave that to some other genius to do, is one of the tragedies of this world. Van Gogh took the impressionist idea of broken color to give light effect, and carried it further, *by drawing in color*, — trying to give both light and form through color, as it has never been done before.

He took the great truth, which I believe El Greco first promoted, of drawing in color, and combined it with the impressionist idea of light. It was a tremendously bold and new undertaking, and when one considers that it was worked out by a man who painted only ten years in all, one realizes the magnitude and penetration of the mind that conceived and developed this idea.

His olive trees, his mountains and rocks, his plowed fields, the last heads and figure-paintings, all show the working out of this thought. But he was unable to carry it to the completion which he sought so passionately to accomplish.

Those whose development in observation has only reached form without knowledge of color will simply be conscious of that crudity of which he himself was aware. Instead of not being able to "think straight," it is the straightest thinking in the matter of color construction the Western world has ever known.

To show the progress of color down the centuries, I need only touch a little more clearly on the difference in color-method between Botticelli and Giorgioni, or the primitive and the man of the Renaissance.

The primitives painted on white ground; the effect they sought was that of light shining through; they sought brilliancy, but every color was within its own outline. As light does not show well over light, they made an underpainting of *terre verte* where heads, hands, or white garments should be on the finished picture.

Giorgione, Titian, Leonardo, and the other masters of the Renaissance, on the contrary, painted on a dark canvas to secure the somber rich effect which they sought. As that excellent technician, Mr. Otto Vermehren, of Florence, said to me, in illustration — "the primitives sought the colors of the sunset, the light shining through, while the later men sought the somber reflected colors of the sunset at the east."

It would simplify the work of many a modern painter if he would use the dark-ground prepared canvases, instead of white or light gray when painting rich and somber pictures.

El Greco, I believe, was the first man to paint in

color and not in outline: that is, in painting the hand, for example, he would be influenced by light and shade or color, his aim being to paint the hand and not the outline of the fingers or the bone construction. His color is very somber, very wonderful in its gradation, and it was very instructive when the big Sonderbund Exhibition in Cologne set aside one room with a very fine example of El Greco and a collection of Van Gogh's paintings in his Brabant period, which are in the same color scheme. It enabled one to see the line of descent, and trace the evolution of Van Gogh's mind to his later great and last period, where he combined the drawing in color with his impressionist picture of light, and gave us that great new thought of color construction in light.

In America little opportunity had been given for studying the modern movement until the recent big International Exhibit this year. We have been reared and trained either in the so-called classic or realistic art, which have produced some of the finest flowers of both the past and the present. But the new branches of art are as legitimate in their way as the two forms already mentioned.

Manet had found his way across the ocean and for a long time has been exercising an influence over the younger painters of this country. Monet, too, left a decided influence; Twacthman and Hassam being the two finest examples — but Pissarro, Renoir, Cezanne, Qauquin, and Van Gogh were hardly more than names. Of the first two, fine examples are to be seen in the

Boston Museum, and in New York. Renoir is to be found also.

The presentation at the recent International Exhibition of the works of these men, with the yet newer movements of Matisse, the Cubist, and the Futurist, caused a confusion of discrimination which is appalling when found in a critic who says, "Post-Impressionist, Cubist, Futurist, however they may be designated, their aim is to turn the world upside down — the one interesting outcome of their common foible is a curious family likeness running through their production." On reading this one feels the effect of a foreigner in a foreign land where all people look alike.

This same critic has well voiced in the following quoted paragraph the lack of understanding of the aims of these earnest painters, who are in the beginning of a new movement in art and not at the completion of it.

"It is, I frankly confess, a difficult if not an impossible task to explain that hypothesis in terms that will be acceptable to the zealots, who, moreover, have always the easy resort that one has not understood their sublime mystery. But I must take the risk and state what after careful study I have gathered to be the Post-Impressionist aim — it is to eschew such approximately accurate representation of things seen as has been hitherto pursued by painters of all schools and to cover the canvas with an arrangement of line and color symbolizing the very essence of the object or scene attacked. For some occult reason it is assumed that a portrait or picture painted according to the familiar grammar of art, understood of all men, is clogged with irrelevant matter. The great masters of the past, to be sure, are not invalidated and they need not be sent to the lumber-room, but their day is done and with the Post-Impressionist we must slough off a quantity of played-out conventions before we can enter the 'Promised Land.'"

After reading such a paragraph, the mind goes back a few hundred years and one has the desire to ask the writer if there is a greater chasm between the past and the present, than there was, at the time of Giotto, between Giotto, Cimabue, and the Byzantine school.

One can easily picture the ardent followers of Byzantine art horrified at the realism Giotto displayed and energetically indorsed, saying, "Why are the followers and admirers of Giotto not content with the familiar grammar of art, understood of all men?" Is it strange that after all these years there should be the swing of the pendulum back from realism to the spirit as best conveyed through formalism? The realism, so splendid in its ascendency, grew until at the end it became mere literal representation — so literal, in fact, that a sitter hardly seemed amazed when she was asked by a well-known portrait painter to secure a bay tree of exact measurements which was needed in the picture as a part of the background. In vain did the sitter search the neighborhood for that special size, and the bay tree had to be abandoned because those secured lacked or exceeded by a few inches the measurement wanted. This story, of course, is extreme, but the rank of the painter made one realize to what extent literalness had grown.

Another outgrowth of this realism is the storytelling picture which has caused untold confusion in the minds of the public in matters relating to art. They confuse the subject with the art standard of the picture. We all know people to whom a religious painting badly painted means more than a fine still-life by a great master. And this confusion is much more prevalent than one at first imagines. Any painter primarily interested in light, color, line, and form can enumerate endless anecdotes where questions were asked which drove him to despair — "What does it mean?" "Why did you paint the figure standing thus or so?" "How strange, I do not see any meaning in that picture!" It is hard to keep constant patience and to explain — especially when these questions are asked by people who are well read in the history of art. It is discouraging to notice how little people use their brains in connection with their eyes — how little they observe. They come to pictures with preconceived ideas of what they wish to see, and if the exhibition is along other lines, they condemn. It is the same in every form of life — people do not like to be disturbed; they love to jog-trot along, enjoying the things in the same everyday way.

Another thing one is conscious of is the confusion as to what constitutes criticism. Criticism should be constructive as well as destructive — the good as well as the bad should be noticed and emphasized. It is illuminating to listen to the conversation in an art gallery or an exhibition. I have often noticed how people will rearrange the composition, perfectly oblivious of the fact that the rearrangement would make a totally different picture — in fact, it became their picture and not the painter's that was being reviewed.

The critic quoted before ends his article with the following paragraph: "Here from the incomplete, halting methods of Cezanne there has flowed out of Paris into Germany, Russia, England, and to some slight extent to the United States, a gospel of stupid license and self-assertion which would be swept into the rubbish heap were it not for the timidity of our mental habit. When the stuff is rebuked as it should be, the Post-Impressionist impresarios and fuglemen insolently proffer us a farrago of supersubtle rhetoric. The farce will end when people look at Post-Impressionist pictures as Mr. Sargent looked at those shown in London, 'absolutely skeptical as to their having any claim whatever to being works of art.'" But is it *quite* fair to Mr. Sargent to end the quotation with a period when it is only a comma? He adds in that famous letter, "with an exception of Gauguin, that strike me as admirable in color and in color only." If Post-Impression is a beginning, a beginning founded essentially *on* color, and one of the leading realists recognizes one of the leaders, is it "timidity" that causes many a person to admire instead of to condemn? And is it within the realm of an artist to be a true critic? If a person is an ardent adherent of one school, can he see as clearly as a nonpartisan the real intrinsic values of all schools — when ideas are intense?

To take an example of another period, when feeling ran high at the time of the Reformation, we now would hardly feel that one could secure an unbiased opinion of the works of a Catholic from a man who was a Protestant, or vice versa. Neither was wholly right, but neither could have accomplished in his own line as much as he did had each not been convinced that his was the only road to salvation. And to ask the opinion or to quote the opinion of a man, who is essentially and brilliantly objective, about a man who is subjective in his work and not the same master of his medium, seems unwise, if what you seek is truth.

I hope that in this Introduction I have in some small measure made clear why in my opinion Van Gogh deserves very serious attention, and have stated it in sufficiently clear and concrete form to prevent it from being called "subtle subterfuge."

Van Gogh has been dead twenty-three years; twenty-three years is a time to be reckoned with.

Rejected in his day and generation by the majority of painters, critics, collectors, and laymen, because he blazed a path into a future in Art which few had the vision to see, and fewer yet to follow, he died because the battle was too constant and his body too weak to stand the strain. Twenty-three years have passed and the vision he sought so passionately is being seen by others until the number of his followers has increased by leaps and bounds. No museum in Holland or Germany finds itself complete without owning his work. So alive is the question in Germany that lawsuits have been waged.

Does all this stand for naught?

Time alone will justify this judgment and this faith, and the truth-seeker will be satisfied. For it is not more fetters, but greater knowledge and freedom that he seeks. "The Truth shall make you free." For out of freedom alone can come the greatest art.

KATHERINE S. DREIER.

June, 1913.

Personal
Recollections
of
Vincent
van Gogh

PERSONAL RECOLLECTIONS

OF

VINCENT VAN GOGH

CHAPTER I

THE PREPARATION

THEY were real village children, playing in the farm garden. Beds of marigolds, mignonette, and brilliant red geraniums were aglow with the setting sun. Everything was in full bloom and athirst for water, this hot late August afternoon. Behind the flower-beds lay the lawn where the snow-white linen was bleached and spread to keep it fresh; next followed row upon row of berry-bushes, rich with the fragrance of the ripening fruit; and the entire garden was inclosed in a beech hedge, which separated it from the fields of rye and grain that stretched beyond as far as the eye could see. In a corner stood a stack of dried peavines with the pods still clinging to them.

Three happy children were clambering up the mound, only to slide down again in greatest glee.

Now and again they stopped a second on their high ground of vantage to survey the surrounding country. Behind them rose the old farmhouse, with its long line of windows, and dark-green shutters, against which the flowers seemed to glow with greater brilliancy. It was a house containing a history — generations had dwelt in it, all of whom had led the same free, unhampered existence; none had known great changes in the even tenor of their lives.

Back of the children stood the house, while stretching out before them as far as the eye could see, lay the fields of rye until lost in a pale gray line on the horizon. There were the meadows and the fruit farms, hardly to be discerned at this great distance, through which a small Brabant stream was gliding under a near-by gleaming white bridge. Speechless the three children — two girls and a boy, of the ages ranging from nine to thirteen — were watching to see who was approaching. Models of spotlessness they certainly were not. The cleanliness of their little frocks and hands left much to be desired. But one forgave them heartily their appearance, for on their faces was the sparkle of childhood and their eyes reminded one of the happiness of the flowers and the freshness of the running stream.

In turning, one of them saw their oldest brother approaching — a boy of seventeen, as broad as he was long, his back slightly bent, with the bad habit of letting the head hang; the red blond hair cropped close was hidden under a straw hat: a strange face, not young; the forehead already full of lines, the eyebrows on the large, noble brow drawn together in deepest thought. The eyes, small and deep-set, were now blue, now green, according to the impressions of the moment. But in spite of all awkwardness and the ugly exterior, one was conscious of a greatness, through the unmistakable sign of the deep inner life.

Brother and sisters were strangers to him as well as his own youth. Hardly matured, his genius was already being felt, though unknown to himself; as a child, who does not understand what its mother is, yet answers at her call.

Without a greeting the brother passed by, out of the garden gate, through the meadows, along the path that led to the stream. The children noted whither he was going, because of the bottle and fishnet he carried. It did not occur to any of them to call after him, "May I come too?" Yet they knew only too well how clever he was at catching the water insects; he would show his trophies to the children on his return. Such jolly little and big beasties! There were broad beetles, with their glossy backs; others with great round eyes, and crooked legs, that nervously wriggled the minute they left the water.

All the beetles, even those with the terrible long feelers, had names, — such horribly long names one could never remember, — and yet their brother knew them all. And then, after he had prepared them, he would carefully pin them in a little box, which first had been beautifully lined with snow-white paper, and neatly labeled with the names pasted above each insect — even the Latin names!

None of the children ever thought of laughing at him: no; he was treated with the deepest respect; but to ask permission to go along to the brook, where it was so deliciously cool, where one could dip one's hands into the sand without soiling one's self — that they did not dare. The most beautiful forget-me-nots grew along the stream, as well as pink water-lilies! The little girls, who loved flowers above everything else, longed for the unattainable!

They were not permitted to leave the garden alone, and on their walks with their parents, it was always, "Children, children, don't go near the water." They felt, however, instinctively, with the delicate sensitiveness of children, that their brother preferred to be alone when home on his vacation from boarding-school. For he sought solitude, not the companionship of his family, and he knew all the places where the rarest flowers grew.

He avoided the little village, with the straight streets and small village houses, out of whose windows the gossips would peep over their curtains with their spectacles tilted on the tips of their noses, and follow the passer-by to see whither he was going. Since the once important little village was no longer the resting-place for the post, where the change of horses was made, it lay as dead and buried. He let it be, and sought instead the woods and fields, watching and studying the life of the underbrush and the birds. The birds he knew intimately; knew where they all lived and had their being, and if he saw a pair of larks descend among the rye, he knew how to watch them closely, without even breaking one fine stalk of grain.

With a thousand voices Nature spoke to him while he listened, but his time had not yet ripened into action.

Not a pen-and-ink drawing, not a pencil sketch of

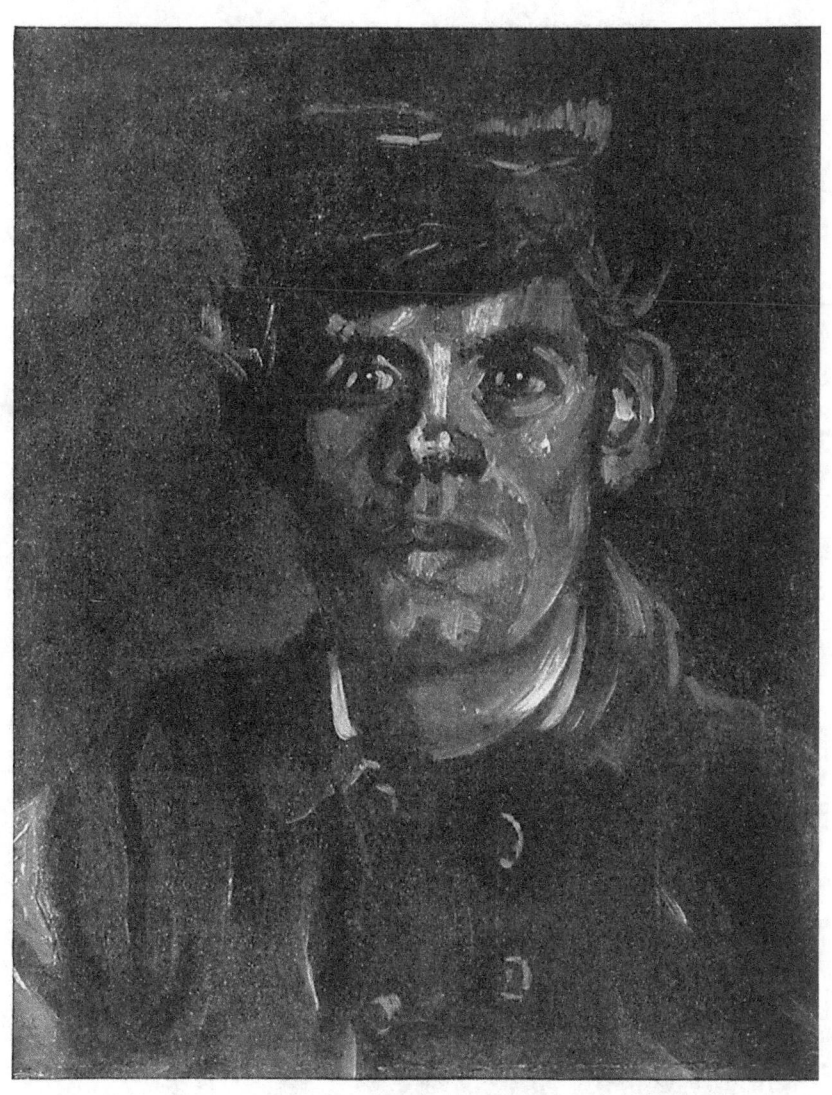

A WORKMAN

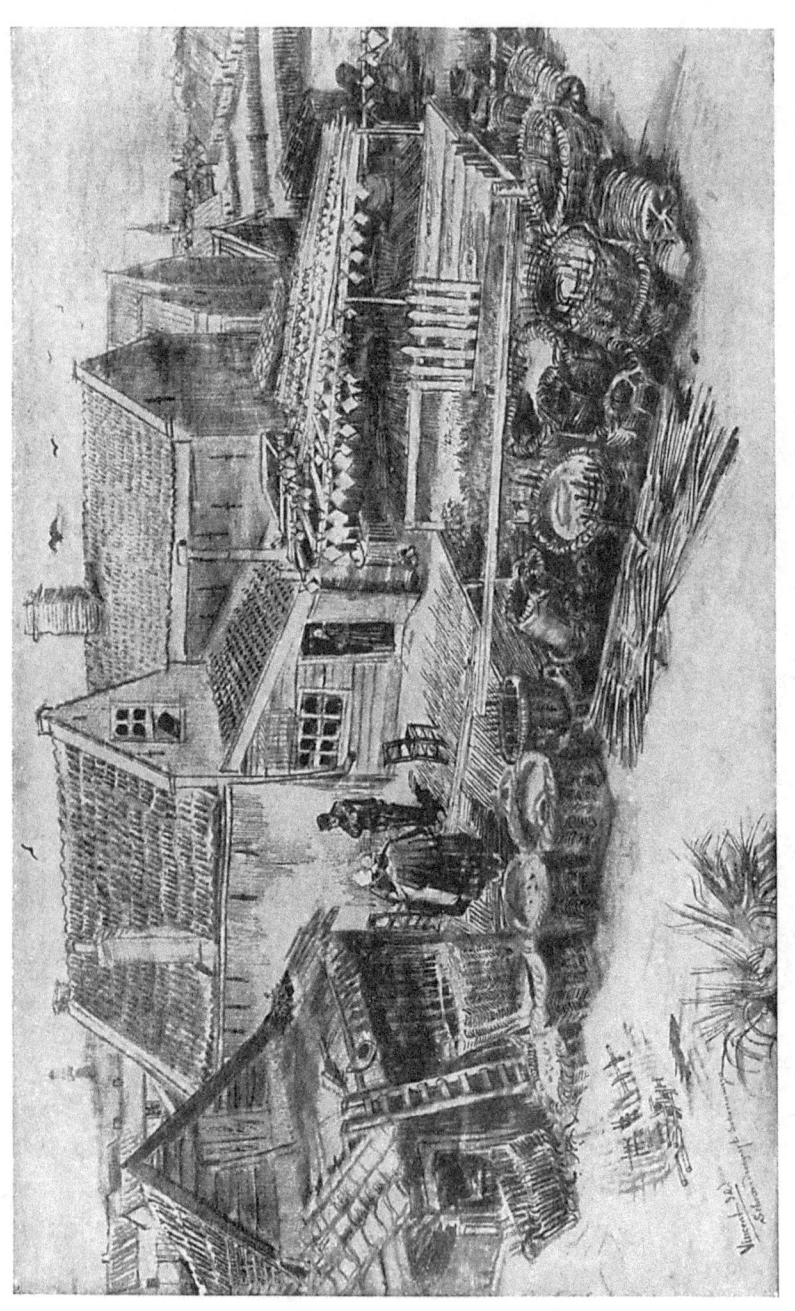

SCHEVENINGEN FISH-HOUSES

this time, exists. He did not think of drawing, the future draughtsman. His mind was given to watching and thinking. When a small boy he modeled an elephant with great accuracy out of some clay which a sculptor's assistant had given him. When eight years old, he surprised his mother by presenting her with a sketch of a cat, who with wild leaps was trying to climb the apple tree in the garden. Surprising as these spontaneous expressions were, even more surprising because they occurred at such rare intervals, they were forgotten, and only remembered years later.

How strong must have been the impressions which cities like The Hague, Brussels, Paris, and London made on this sensitive personality from the country! Often, years afterwards, those dormant impressions would waken to some spontaneous form of line and color under totally different aspects, even outwardly taking other shapes. Yet one can trace them back to these first impressions. And possibly it was this long slumbering impression of Paris which years later produced "Marseille," as it stretches along with its sharp contours against the dark-blue heavens, with its thousand lights streaming out from the town and harbor, trying to conquer the brilliancy of the stars above. The conviction with which this brilliancy was accomplished may never again be attained in art.

. . . .

His school-days were ended. The Director of the Academy had wished the parents success and happiness in the future of their gifted son. And following family tradition, Vincent Van Gogh was now to become a merchant.

Formerly, as now, it was considered a special favor for a young man, who wished to become an art dealer, to receive his training from Goupil, who had made the business a world-wide enterprise by establishing houses in Berlin, New York, and London, besides having connections in The Hague and Brussels. First at The Hague and then at Brussels, he received his training. Later he was to go to Paris. The duties of an apprentice were similar to those in a bookshop — to pack or unpack, to develop and have under his charge all photographs and 'reproductions of well-known pictures, or even to lend a hand in the boxing of paintings.

With all these tasks he was content. He had a dexterity which one would not have suspected from his rough exterior. It had been noticed already, when, as a child, he so carefully handled his collection of beetles; or in the tying and arranging of flowers; and later in his great natural gift of nursing the sick. Without a murmur he performed all these humble duties which were really beneath a man of his knowledge of art and literature, yet all the more gladly he seemed to do them, because he felt that they were aiding him in his preparation as a painter.

Art of the most varying kind came to his hand: art from all the ruling countries of the world, pictures and their reproductions by all sorts of artists. As heretofore he had been absorbed in Nature, so now he became deeply engrossed in studying how she was reproduced. Often it seemed to him that the picture did not reproduce the Nature he knew and loved so well, with the sincerity and truth due her. He also noticed that praise was not always given where, according to his knowledge, praise seemed due. It astonished, troubled, and angered him.

"Que voulez-vous? C'est la mode" was the answer given him as he hesitatingly told his opinion to a fellow-assistant. It was Fashion, then, that dictated the laws in the Realm of Beauty — Fashion, which he scorned — Fashion put her stamp of "to be or not to be" on the works of an artist and determined the fate of those who belonged to him. She it was who gathered unto herself these treasures or threw them aside with scorn, and banished the creator to a poverty which could cripple his ability forever. And he should become her slave and kneel at her feet to pay her homage, — he who had never felt any need for society, who was a stranger to her laws and her convention! He should help to throw sand into the eyes of the public, spoil good taste knowingly, and in this way help to destroy what was truly fine — that would, indeed, suit him!

As an art dealer, an educated young man could always find a secured future. But though he was modest, as most great men are, he had never taken the slightest notice of what the world calls "form." He was perfectly unconscious of having distressed his parents, in that he never joined the happy family group, never met people, but always sought solitude. The sending home of his first earnings, after he had been advanced to Paris, proved to his family that this aloofness was only an inability to give himself, even to those he loved.

Shortly after receiving this gift from their son, his parents received word from the firm that they were very sorry to say that while he gave absolute satisfaction at first while at The Hague and in Brussels, especially on the practical side, they were compelled to inform them that his awkwardness and shyness were a detriment to him in his business which threatened to become insurmountable. Personal peculiarities of this kind were particularly disturbing to the Parisians — especially to ladies, who, being convinced of their own knowledge of art, did not care to be corrected by this "rustre Hollandais," as they termed him. Were it not for the connection which his family had with one of the heads of the firm, he would long ago have been dismissed. They were sending him to London to see whether it were not possible to meet the situation in that way, as it might be easier for him to have dealings with the English.

This news was like a bolt out of a clear sky, for though the parents were not blind to the peculiarities of their eldest son, they were yet so accustomed to hear him praised that it was hard to realize that he could be so careless about his future as to destroy it so ruthlessly.

Their depression was great, when, six weeks later, they received word from him that he had received his final dismissal. A quarrel had occurred between him

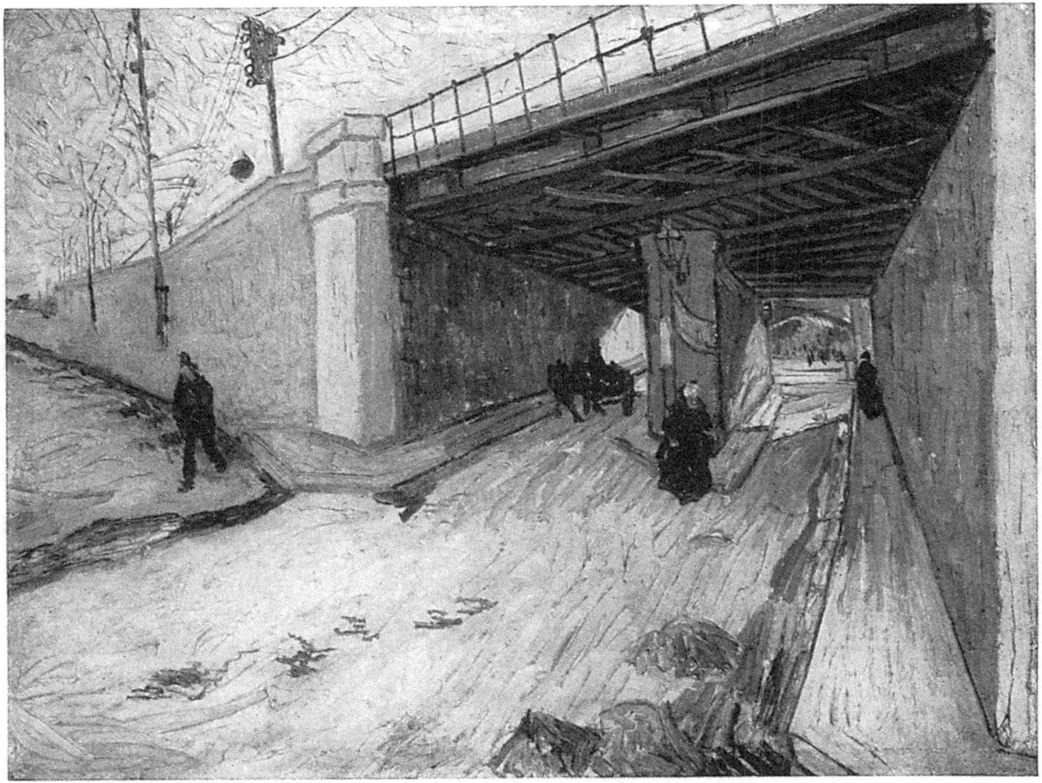

THE ROAD UNDER THE RAILWAY

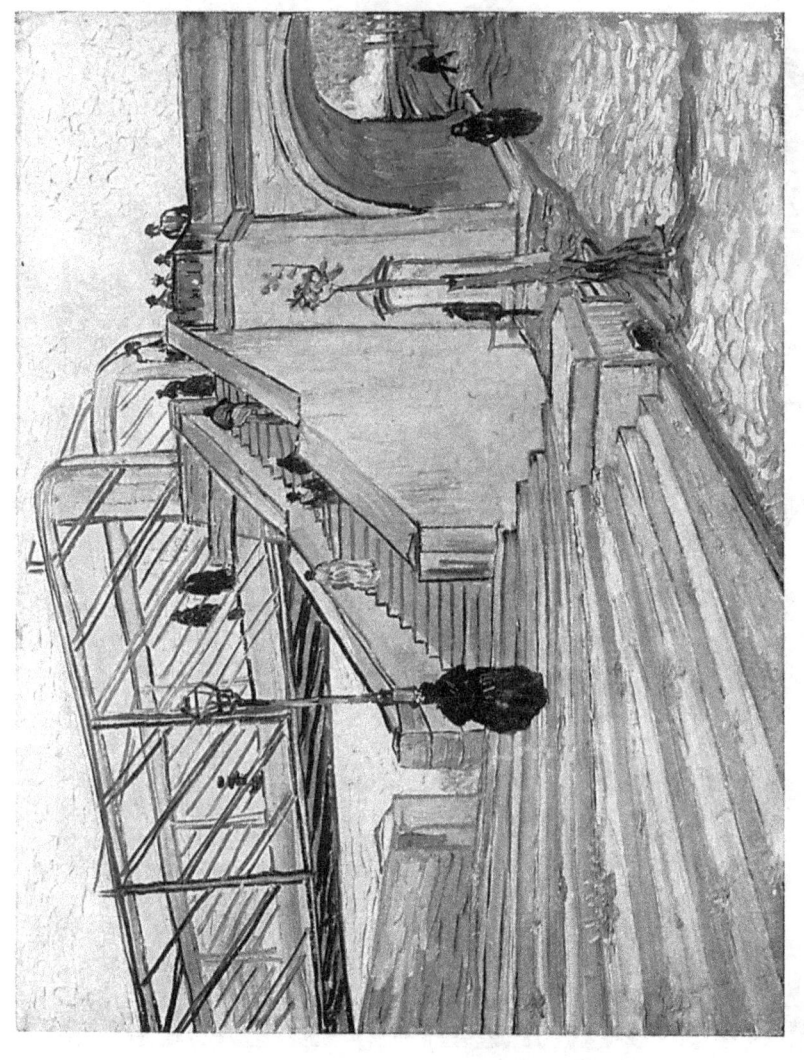

THE BRIDGE OVER THE RAILWAY

and his London chief in which he had clearly told the latter his opinion: that bargaining was seeking to get the better of another, which was simply legitimate stealing and that he would not stand for it. Because of his honesty, he had received his dismissal. His parents need not be troubled over the matter. One month's salary had been paid in advance, besides which he had looked for a situation and had already found one; thus he wrote.

A vicar had established a boarding-school, to eke out the pittance which did not meet his daily needs for himself and his large family, and wanted the young man to teach French.

The shyness which one felt in his speech did not show itself in his home letters. He wrote often and in great detail. His style was halting and abrupt, as if a deep impression had to rest awhile within his heart before it could find expression. With the stroke of a real artist, along big human lines, he would depict exquisite landscapes, sunny corners, street scenes, etcetera, comparing them with scenes at home, thereby making them real and concrete. Sometimes with a few lines he would sketch figures to illustrate more clearly his thought. Later, when writing about paintings on which he was working, he would illustrate them with pen-and-ink drawings.

In a letter to his parents he gave a description of his present situation in the neighborhood of London. He described the vicar as a long, lean man, bent with the care of his large family, whose needs his small earnings in no wise met, and who, so to speak, just hung in his clothes. His face was heavily lined, and the color of some wooden-looking saint in an old picture. The wife he described as a quiet, delicate little woman, with eyes as blue as the early March violets.

There were twenty boarders in the old gray vicarage which was overgrown with clematis and roses. Nevertheless, the interior furnishing resembled one of Dickens's descriptions of a school, so cleverly caricatured in the Chapman & Hall edition. The boys appeared as if they had stepped out of these illustrations, especially when, on a Sunday afternoon, in their short jackets, long trousers, and high hats, after the service, where they had sung in the choir, they played leapfrog — boys between eleven and sixteen, lean and pale, caricatures of their youth — "Mr. Creakle's young gentlemen, as they appear enjoying themselves."

Again, though hardly as a surprise, it was found that the young man had little talent for his new-chosen duty. His pupils did not torment him. His troubles were not those of Mr. Mell in "David Copperfield," a subject of torment and a person to be scorned, for he always knew how to awaken respect. Besides, over those of his pupils whose mentality was a little more developed than the rest, he knew how to cast a spell with tales of Holland, the land without hills and of many rivers, where the houses and streets were as clean and spotless as the play-toys of the giants in "Gulliver's Travels." As a teacher of languages he served little purpose. His growing genius rebelled to find itself in fetters. He suffered greatly from the narrow limits of his field of work, and the ever regular recurring duties, to which he could never quite accustom himself.

Most of the scholars belonged to the very lowest class of small London shopkeepers, sons of small butchers, if one may give them the dignified name of butchers; men who bought and sold meat that reputable firms had refused to purchase; sons of cobblers or of small shopkeepers, where notions or tobacco were sold. The children were generally sent to school because of their health, or because of the numerous ones at home, without considering whether the small income could meet this extra expense.

If the money were not forthcoming at the close of the term, steps were often taken to collect these payments first by personal calls upon the parents, before sending the pupils away or even taking sharper measures. To this undesirable task of collecting outstanding school debts, the principal now assigned his young teacher. It was in all probability the most distasteful duty, to one of his temperament, that the young man had yet been asked to perform.

However, stuffing a map of London and the needed addresses in his pocket, he set forth, with just enough money to meet his bare expenses. Knowing London thoroughly, and being used to poking around odd corners, he soon found the desired families, even those who had moved, or, worse still, had given false addresses. The debtors, being unprepared for this visit, paid, and the vicar was indeed gratified, as he had never before collected so fully all that was due him.

If it was not the very lowest section of the city the young teacher visited, they certainly were back streets and alleys to which he had to go, where the struggle for life had emaciated the bodies, bent the backs, and left relentless lines on drawn and pinched faces. Who knows but that the poverty witnessed here imprinted on the future painter's imagination the desire to picture it upon canvas, and gave to the world, years later, in his Brabant period, the "Aardappeleeters," where a workingman's family is seated around the evening meal of a dish of potatoes.

If the vicar congratulated himself on the ability of his young teacher to collect debts, he certainly met with disappointment with the returns from the second attempt. Prepared to meet him, these small shopkeepers told such tales of woes that were pressing upon them that it seemed as if no chance for happiness were left. Instead, they seemed to kill, in a far greater measure than the most sordid need he had met with in the country. The heart of the young Dutchman bled at the sorrow he beheld — parents who dragged out a miserable life like gray shadows, through grayer streets, without fresh air, a life full of burdens for the body as well as the soul; children who never knew the meaning of the word "youth," but came into the world with the gray, drawn faces of old men.

Full of keen sympathy for all the sorrow he had seen,

THE " AARDAPPELEETERS "

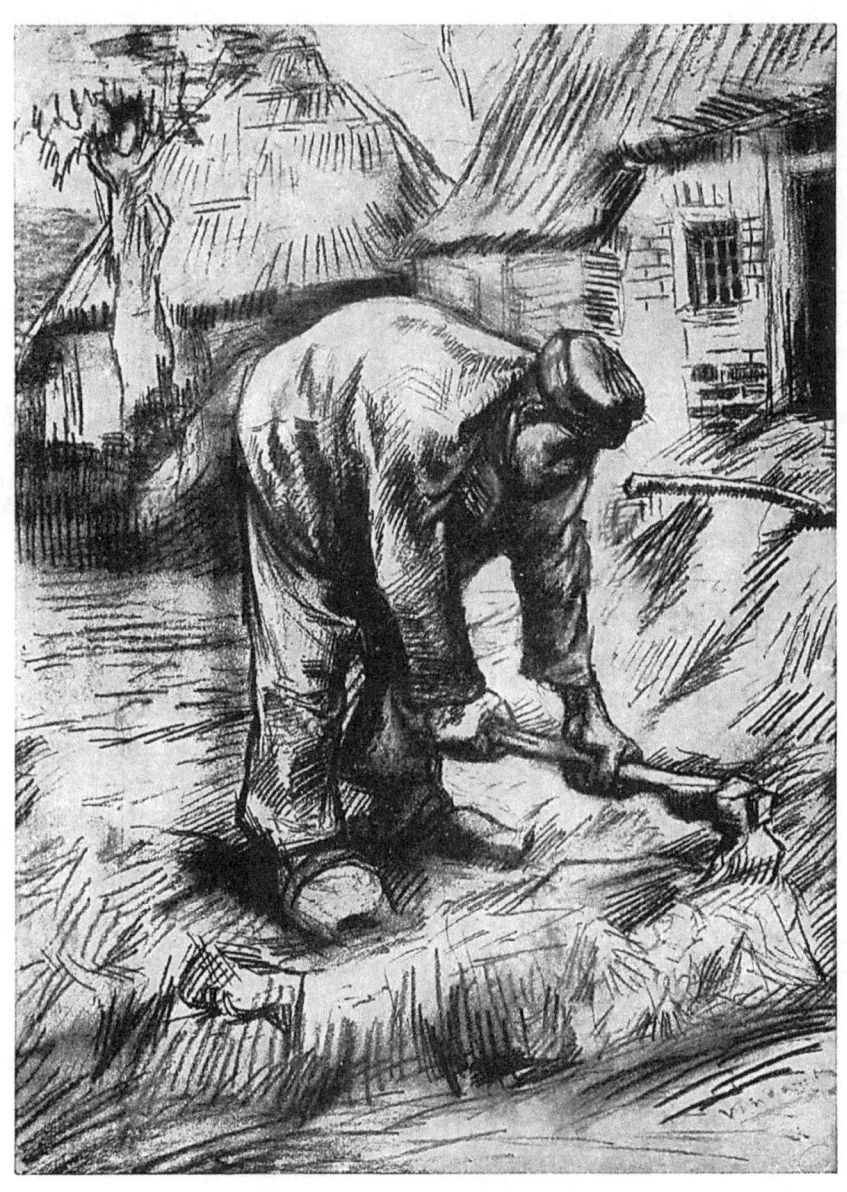

THE FARM LABORER

he forgot the mission he had come for, and returned with empty purse and a heart full of woe. On his return he told of the heartrending things he had seen, but was again and again interrupted, for the vicar's only interest lay in the amount he had succeeded in collecting from these miserable people. When, therefore, he heard of the empty purse, he flew into such a rage that he dismissed his young assistant on the spot.

With worn boots, and no outlook, the young teacher returned to the home of his parents. Great was their disappointment — greater their fear for his future. Only too well did they realize that all this misfortune was due to his awkwardness, as his mother was wont to call it.

However, fortune favored him and a position was soon secured in a well-known bookshop. Being a great reader, his knowledge of literature and foreign languages made him a valued asset to the firm.

Even greater attraction than his new-found work did the old Dutch town hold for him, with its quaint character and its lovely scenery. One street especially had great charm for him; for from a certain point it looked exactly as it must have done three hundred years ago. Especially entrancing was the view overlooking the broad stream, alongside of which he lived. On the opposite shore stretched the broad meadows; in the distance buildings and towers rose high above the horizon, and the stream itself ever changed color, according to wind and weather, sunshine and clouds mirroring themselves in it. The river carried many crafts of all kinds

and descriptions, a sight that has constantly aroused
painters to try their mettle. But the time, for him, was
not yet ripe.

His apprenticeship had not been served. The master-
craft lay in the distant future, as far removed from the
present time as the distant towers on the horizon. His
genius had not yet awakened, but unconsciously was
working all the time towards its final goal. Always
observing and alert, as those others who work at their
own development in their own special way, there is
nothing strange in what he achieved when once he began to paint; it is not surprising that he should develop
more rapidly and accomplish more within ten years
than others achieve in a lifetime. People have mar-
veled over this, those who have written about him.
But as they talked about one they did not know,
and only listened to the sound of their own voices, they
did not consider, or were unable to grasp, all that
was developing in the painter during these preceding
years.

A quiet apprentice-shop was the museum that bears
the name of Ary Scheffer, and his art treasures, especially the works by Scheffer himself, a jewel in the crown
of the old town of Dordrecht. Never, even with his
tremendous colors, would Vincent have succeeded as he
did, had he not first thoroughly studied the works of
Ary Scheffer, teacher of the children of Louis Philippe,
who was thoroughly acquainted with the old and the
modern French paintings, and who had sought to
achieve through exactness and delicacy of drawing what

his admirer sought to gain through vigor, greater simplicity, and the use of contrasting colors.

In the bookshop where he was engaged, he could satisfy his craving for knowledge. His employer had recognized that the young man was exceptionally gifted, as did every one who came in personal touch with him, and allowed him the use of his most valuable books. This increased his knowledge. A clergyman — one could more readily call him a scholar — at whose house he was made welcome, and where he would often go to enjoy a scholarly disputation, told Vincent's family, whom he knew well, that he was amazed that so talented a young person did not attend the university. With his insight into human nature, and his deep, true outlook on life, surely he would forge ahead of all others as soon as the opportunity was given him to devote his entire time to his studies. Of course, he was not normal, but great men seldom were.

Hope reawakened in the hearts of his parents. A new future seemed again to be opening for their eldest-born. In the mean time, the second son had accepted a position at Goupil's, where Vincent had all but failed. The same opportunities were offered to this brother, for whom one could predict success.

After all, might these early trials not have been the wrong turnings on the road of life, and antagonistic to his real nature, which sought seclusion and introspection?

An uncle, a brother of his father, stationed at the

Navy Yard at Amsterdam, offered the young man the hospitality of his home during the year of preparation for the university. He paid for his nephew's tuition in the study of the ancient languages, which were needed to pass the entrance examination. Within a few months Vincent had mastered both Latin and Greek, under the guidance of a Jewish rabbi, who, though young at the time, had already won a reputation for himself as a scholar.

In the mean time, the parents dreamt their dreams of the future, in the small border village of Brabant, far from the turmoil of the large cities. They are not forgotten, this honored couple, in the small world in which they lived in undisturbed married felicity spinning threads of love and loyalty around the hearts of their neighbors. When one thinks of them, one is tempted to quote from Horace, "Disturbed by no ill word, our love lasts until death."

Often one could see them on their way to visit the sick in all stations of life and to render help. Regardless of bad weather or worse roads, walking along the countryside, across fields or down paths that were skirted by hedges, or following the dykes and moats: two dark figures in the lonely landscape, now and then stopping to emphasize a point in some lively discussion which they were holding, or to notice the beauty in the landscape — the silver edge of a cloud, or the last rays of the sun, glorifying the heavens; a pool made mysterious through the dark reflection of somber pines, yet mirroring back a glint of the blue sky; or the lonely farm which they had been seeking, where dwelt the invalid they had come to succor; a farm with all the happy and comfortable whirr of farm life, which only the real country offers. Picturesquely it lay there in the landscape, with its simple straight lines, and masses of color. There they would stand for a moment together, neither of them tall, but straight and conscious — he with finely chiseled features, set in silver locks, not suited to his age; she with less even features and the wide-awake, alert look of deep-seeing eyes which her eldest son had inherited: a perfect couple, such as one finds portrayed in the early English novels, or sees pictured in those splendid English engravings of that same period.

Naturally, the fate of their six children was often under discussion. The eldest daughter, with her father's fine features but the blond hair and coloring of the mother, was in England, completing her education. Her future seemed assured. The second son, who had inherited his father's name and goodness of heart, was in Paris. The three youngest were children who still needed their mother's care and forethought. It was always the eldest son whose welfare mostly concerned them. It was as if a still, small voice was whispering to them all that which was ripening within him, and which only the mother lived to see fulfilled.

In spite of their great modesty they loved to dwell on the past and to recall special figures in it. The father,

who was well informed concerning such matters, would
tell his wife of one who, hundreds of years ago, had
borne the same name; he had been Bishop of Utrecht.
Madame Bosboom Tousaint mentions him in her his-
torical romance, "Elizabeth Musch." Another, a
knight, was treasurer of the United General States,
and brought honor to the family name during the siege
of Hertogenbosh, under Frederick Henry. Yet another
had been ambassador to England under William III.
Apparently the love of study was once more manifest-
ing itself in their eldest son.

Already their dreams were to be shattered on this
same rock. During the time that the young man was
preparing for his examinations, he had a mental break-
down. While studying, he not only spent half the night
working, but wrote so incessantly that at last the
writing was no longer legible on the closely written
sheets, and became mere pen-strokes without rhyme
or reason — nothing more. The flame had burned too
fiercely. A glimmering flame always, it was now ready
to break forth at any moment to destroy him.

His uncle and host had nothing to offer in the way
of companionship. His public as well as his private life
was lived with military precision. Punctual, and with
an inordinate love for order, he had taken this strange
nephew into his home only to please the latter's parents.
The young man was served separately and he took no
further notice of him.

Nor was any notice of him altogether possible, for the
young man wandered about the old town and the back

streets at all hours of the day and night. Sundays he would attend six or seven churches or meetings. To the synagogues he would also go, to study their form of service and the old Hebrew laws which are the basis of the new laws Christ established. How much his nervous system was unstrung is revealed by the fact that at one time he threw his silver watch into the collection plate; at another time his gloves. The watch was marked with his monogram and name, and was returned to his uncle's house.

The great number of home letters he wrote at this time caused his parents to shake their heads. Sometimes two would arrive the same day, and if the mail brought one late, it generally meant a sleepless night.

It was a bitter disappointment when their son informed his parents, just as his term at the university was to begin, that he felt called upon to preach the Gospel, without further preparation. Christ Himself was his example. He had attended lectures under the Pharisees and Sadducees, and so had the Apostles. During the stay in England, Vincent had heard much about mission work among the miners. One of Dickens's books had awakened in him a deep sympathy for the people who spent half their lives in the dark, as well as under great danger. While reading this description, his sympathetic heart had felt called upon to do its share to relieve the suffering. Shortly after this decision he offered his services and was called to the Borinage, the well-known coal-fields of Belgium, where the need for the Gospel was great. A small wooden church had not yet been erected, as there were no means, but a large room or barn could be found.

Despite their great desire to see their son in a secure post, the parents gave their consent to this plan, for the great need and praiseworthy motive had to be acknowledged.

That his parents were suffering financially because of him he was quite unconscious of, though it was just at this period that his father appeared to him as his ideal. For the present his parents could do nothing but see that all his needs were met for his new position, and to send a trunk filled with what his mother had sewn and knitted with her own hands, works of love, tenderest mother-love woven in with the threads.

How could a real artist soul, such as his was, place itself in the midst of such terrible suffering? I have often thought that the source of all true art is real human love, a love which has to express itself again and again. Every new work is a sacrifice to this love for mankind, to bring to it new hope in its sorrow, new strength for the battle. There, where Art appears on holy ground, she appears to me at her highest, in remembrance of the great Sacrifice, the complete giving of Him who surely realized to the full the god-quality in Art.

How these types of miners must have impressed themselves upon the future painter, the faces lined and withered, — never fresh and blooming as are those of other people, who also must earn their living by the sweat of their brows, but can do so under God's own

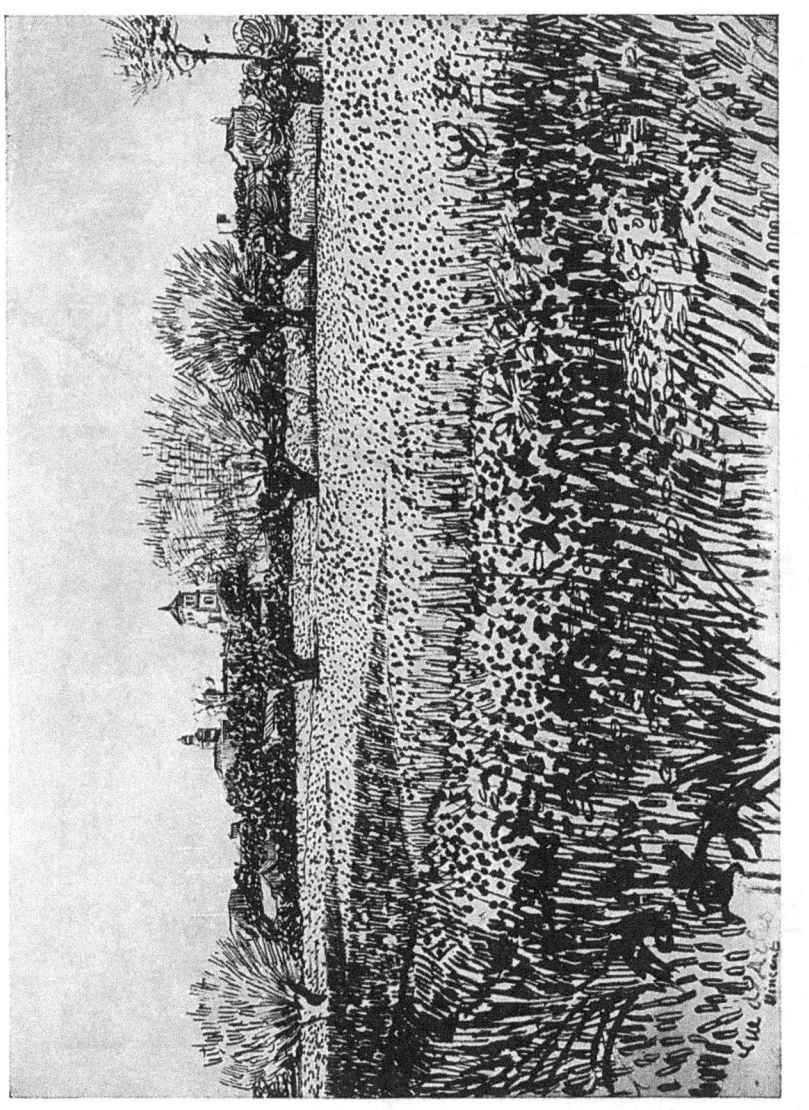

A VIEW OF ARLES

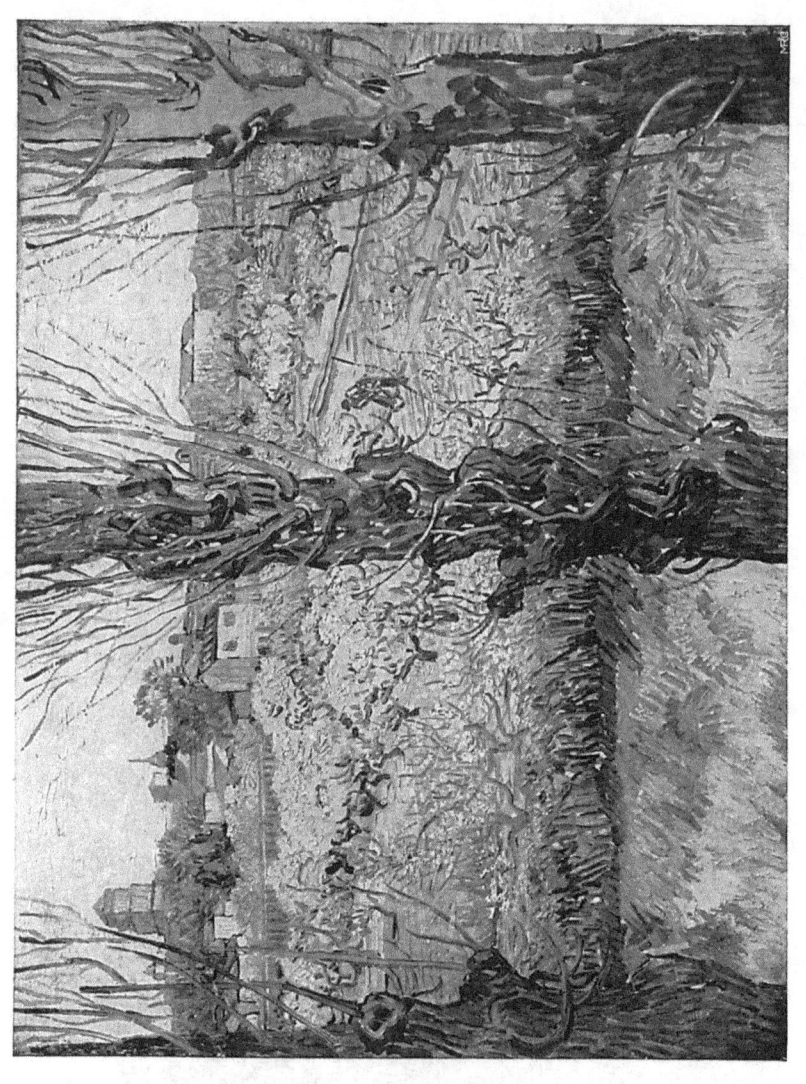

A VIEW OF ARLES

sun, when it breaks forth through the early morning mist, until the twilight steals along!

The women of the Borinage in their unattractive dress, the head wrapped in a black kerchief to protect it against the coal dust, were, almost without exception, thin, ugly, and old before their time. Occasionally one saw a maiden or a young matron who seemed like some glorified being in spite of her tragic surroundings; like a lily in all its purity, which has grown to the glory of God; or the apparition of an angel, or the memory of the Eve of Paradise.

With a baker, a little better situated than the rest, the young Hollandaise found quarters. A large workshop with red-brick flooring and blackened beams, which joined the baker's shop and was heated from it, was chosen for the religious meetings. The baker's family consisted of father, mother, and three splendid sons, who faithfully attended all the services. The rest of the audience consisted of a small group of miners, who came irregularly, but since the arrival of our friend came rather more often than less. The preaching had been in French and was the language chosen. This was no obstacle, since Vincent spoke and wrote French as if it were his mother tongue. He was no orator, although the manners of a speaker were his. The quick, telling gesticulation of his hands with which he would emphasize a point in his stories — stories told with the same simplicity his mother had used when telling them to him as a child — gripped the hearts of his unlettered listeners, and brought food and renewed vigor to the

brain which had become exhausted through the heavy
physical labor of the day.

Although no serious accident occurred during the
period that Vincent was in the Borinage, no day passed
which did not record some minor mishaps, and soon it
became customary to turn to the missionary for the
needed help of having one's wounds dressed.

I was anticipating when I spoke elsewhere of his
great dexterity and almost feminine tenderness in
nursing, which found its fullest expression when a ty-
phoid epidemic broke out among the miners. Their
numbers lessened — no one was spared. Old and young
suffered alike, and it was then that the baker's wife
wrote, in her firm round hand, to the parents, and told
them in her simple fashion of the terrible conditions
which existed; how merciless the sickness had been; how
great the poverty was; and that "le jeune Monsieur
qui n'était pas comme toutes autres" had given everything to relieve the suffering. He had moved into a
lonely, empty hut to save all personal expense, thereby
being able to give even more; and everything he owned,
in the way of clothing or money, he had sacrificed to the
poor. Day and night he had nursed them, and had not
left their bedside. She herself had sons and was a
mother, and, therefore, she had written the parents,
who would know nothing, and would believe their son
well cared for in her home.

As usual, the mail was late in bringing the letter.
Silently the mother had listened to the reading, silently

had husband and wife stood together at its close, both fearful to express their thoughts to each other.

"The best thing will be for me to go there to-morrow and bring him back myself," the father said, at last. The pressure of his hand was all the mother was able to give him at that time. After a long, dreary, sleepless night, all the difficulties of the journey were discussed, but they were all banished by the overwhelming desire to have their beloved son safe once more.

Everything was as the good baker's wife had said. In a forsaken hut, a straw sack for a bed, a jacket for a cover, the father found his son. Broken under the heavy strain of nursing and the renunciation of even the bare necessities of life, he soon consented to return home with his father. The baker's eldest son had to promise him to continue the services. The father spent the night with these hospitable and kindly people, and a service was held before their departure the next day. The quiet hour left an impression on both which was never to be forgotten. A handful of miners, ravaged by hunger and sickness, followed with deep attention the service, which was read by one of their own number. The hanging lamps cast fantastic shadows against the whitewashed walls, and threw across the ceiling curious shapes and forms. Yet over the faces of these miners a light was shining, as they attended, which was not of earth, but seemed of heaven beyond.

CHAPTER II

THE BEGINNING

AT last, as a stream overcomes all obstacles and finds its true course to the ocean, so the genius of Van Gogh found its medium of expression. The young man began to paint.

He showed his family sketches he had done of the miners. These were not many, for his time had been too full of other work. But it was a beginning, and what he drew was alive: a miner in front of his hut, which resembled greatly the low huts in Brabant, with the extremely high straw-thatched roofs; old and over-grown with moss and evergreen, as full of color as a mosaic; a miner and his wife haggard, with arms and legs which seemed too long, because of their thinness, the clothing worn, worn the faces, each carrying a heavy sack of coal upon the back. With long strides they were walking homeward, along a path not made of earth, but of coal dust; everything poor, cold, and dirty.

From a well-known firm brushes and paints were ordered, and a few months later he left for Antwerp, to attend the art school. It must have been in February or March that he went.

One Sunday afternoon the end of May saw him back most unexpectedly. His sisters seated by the window with their embroidery saw him running up the path that led to the house, dressed in a workingman's blouse, such as the Flemish cattlemen wear, the felt hat pulled deep down over his forehead, a big easel strapped to his back. He wished to stay with his parents, and the village offered many subjects for him to work at. It was not the picturesque part of Brabant, and the inhabitants were not friendly toward artists and did not meet them halfway, as is so necessary to enable them to do their best work.

One can acknowledge without fear his work at this period as uncouth and faulty, excepting his flowers. Whether they belong to his early or late period, they always bear the quality of their own special character, and for a long time they were his own special pictures. "Plants radiant with life in tender, quivering form, shy as silken butterflies." So have Vincent's flowers been described. But in his heart he rather chose Wordsworth's words, —

"To me the deepest flower that blows can give
Thoughts that do often lie too deep for tears."

The parents of the painter were bombarded with questions from well-meaning friends and relatives.

Alas, in our state of society, though it surely is not a pleasing custom, each one presumes to have the right to pass judgment upon a fellow-being, and feels called upon to offer advice, especially with the bringing-up of children. "If that were my son, or my daughter, I would" — and then follows exactly the opposite of what the parents had deemed or chosen as the wisest measure.

"If I were as wealthy as these people, I would surely or I would surely not, etc.," — and then follows something which again contradicts itself. And so in this case a hundred tongues let themselves be heard, each with a different opinion, and every one was, of course, convinced that to follow his special advice would be the best for Vincent.

It would never do for a young man of twenty-eight not to support himself. He ought to be treated differently. He should be made to dress better, to go among people instead of shunning them, to behave like others (as if it were not a privilege to be one's self and not like every one else). His father should be more severe, and if that did not help, send him to an institution, etc., etc. This was the form the good advice took. As if the parents had not suffered sufficiently to find themselves robbed of all their fond hopes, besides the ever growing financial difficulties which were pressing upon them. The technique of their son demanded much paint, and paint is expensive. To add to their disappointment, they in no way admired his work. What they liked he scorned, and what satisfied him was in their eyes bad taste. His intercourse with them at this time was not of the easiest.

Around Christmas-time he silently disappeared and in no happy frame of mind, leaving the parents full of sorrow and uncertainty as to where he had gone. They believed he had returned to England, when they received word from him that he had decided to work in The Hague. He had visited his Cousin Mauve, who

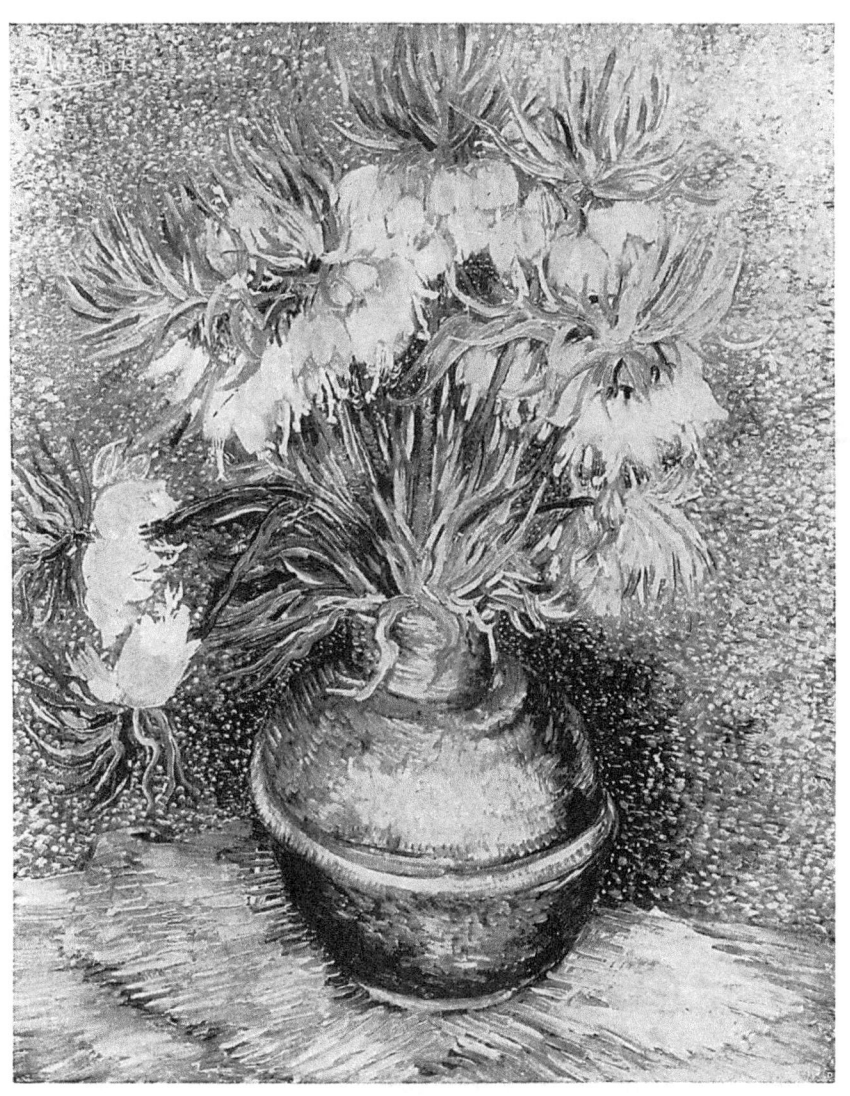

FLOWERS

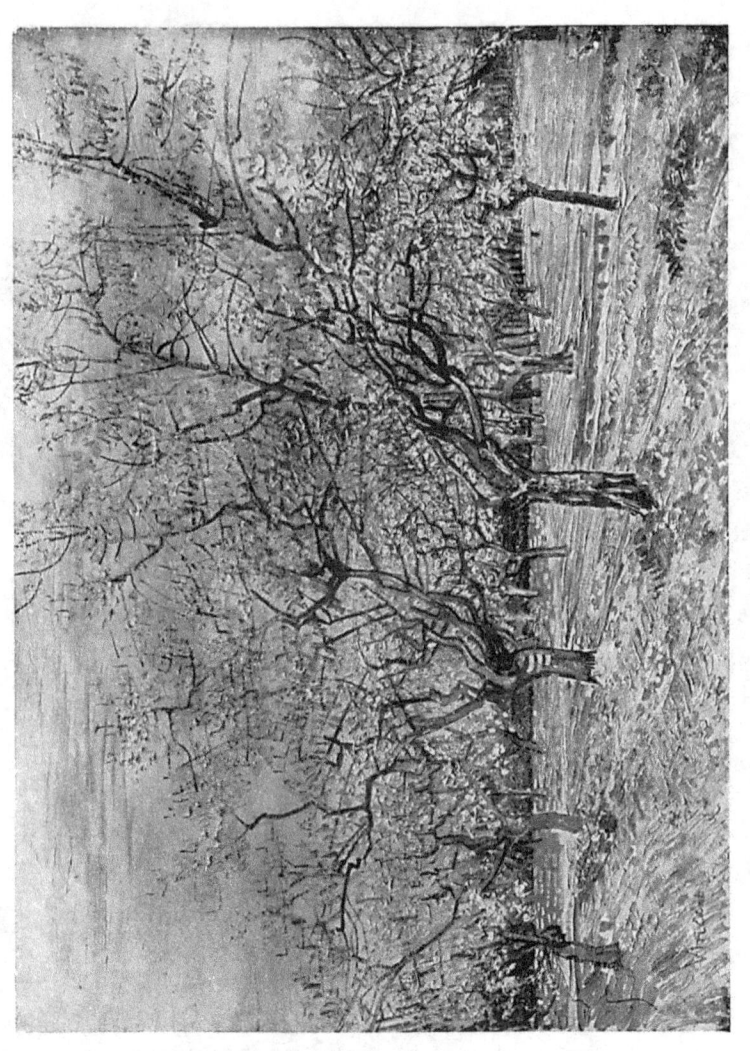

FLOWERING OLIVE TREES

offered to let him work in his studio, and his Cousin
Ariette, — Mauve's wife, — whom he later presented
with his "Apple Blossoms," gave him a warm welcome
in their home.

Now he could feel himself grow. The art school at
The Hague, whose members he knew personally,
gripped him: Mauve, through his tender and poetic
interpretation of small beech lanes, stretches of heather
plains, with the shepherd and his sheep, the only living
features in the quiet of the landscape, whose serenity
they never disturbed; fields and beech hedges, which
kept the autumn's red-brown leaves until the breaking
of the spring, whose approach one felt in the picture,
— how carefully he had studied Nature!

The pictures of Maris, with their fresh dexterity
and sureness of the first brush stroke, interested him;
also Gabriel, de Bock, and Pozzenbeck, and the master
of all, Israels. With quiet sureness he absorbed the best
as was his wont, never becoming an imitator, but always holding himself aloof. When Mauve advised him
to draw after a plaster cast, and arranged a figure for
him in his studio with artificial light, he threw it down,
in spite of the danger of breaking it, and disappeared
from the studio.

Naturally this incident destroyed the friendship, for
Mauve, who was nervous and excitable, could not
tolerate such behavior. Vincent could never see any-
thing but the humorous side, and as often as he would
tell it, he would laugh over it, as a street gamin does
over a successful joke. Strange as it may seem, it never

lessened his admiration for Mauve. He feared every influence that might force itself upon him and cause him
to become an imitator or to lean on others; he did not
wish to follow a school.

"Honesty toward one's self is the supreme law for
a painter, and alone brings to full fruition the inspira-
tion he holds. In contrast, haste and dishonesty toward one's self end in self-seeking." This, Mr. Plaes-
schart said in the "Groene Amsterdamer" of February
27, 1910.

These artists stood together; he stood alone — alone
in his work.

In the autumn of 1908, at the Paris exhibition, — so
an eye-witness relates, — there were people who stood
speechless with admiration before his work, while
others, shrugging their shoulders, would exclaim, turning, "C'est un fou."

Long before the artist had a name, the painter
Gabriel asked a lady, in whose company he acciden-
tally saw one of Vincent's paintings, "And what do you
think of his art?" She, who was no painter, did not
venture to express an opinion, and so answered, "I am
glad that you call it art, Mr. Gabriel"; whereupon the
master laughed good-naturedly.

That his pictures were scorned by the art dealers,
and, therefore, could find no market, did not disturb
him at all. That a well-known art critic refused to ac-
cept one of his flower pieces, simply on the condition

that it should be hung in his collection, caused him to laugh. His art carried him on eagle wings, above the pettiness of this world, and had any one wished to reproach him with the thought that at his age he was not even self-supporting, he would surely have answered, as did He whose life is above all, when his parents reproached him for remaining behind among the doctors and learned men, a boy of twelve, "Do you not know that I must be about my Father's business?"

"Ils vivent, les yeux tournés vers le dedans," to quote from Taine's "History of English Literature."

Genius must develop by overcoming hard obstacles through its power of love for its work, otherwise it will always remain like a diamond hidden in the quartz which surrounds it and which prevents the sun's rays from reflecting back its beauty.

Did the young man have the opportunity of observing the untiring work of the miner; did he recall with what energy the reapers swung their sickles through the rye, or their scythes through the high grass during the long summer evenings when a coming storm on the horizon drove the men to redouble their energy in gathering in the crop before the storm broke forth? Now had his time arrived for work.

At night he would study books on water-color and perspective. During the day he visited museums or studios, drew from models, or copied a whole series of French cartoons, which were very instructive, because of the lifelike qualities of the figures done in simple outline, which bespoke a mastery of linework which more than repaid the trouble of copying. These studies inspired him to do a series of his own, from models. They are not the least noteworthy of the work, especially one, a woman. The picture is all the more telling because of its great simplicity. Spare, and aged before her time, the head with the thin, straight hair, bent low over the scrawny knees, there she sits bare and lonely; with characteristic lettering the deep-meaning word "Sorrow" was placed on the margin. This picture needs special mention, for it always recalls to my mind the little poem of Josef Cohen: —

> "Through all the centuries down,
> There stands in a lonely alley
> Lonely a woman.
> Her garments speak of joy,
> Her eyes tell of sorrow."

Especially this: —

> "Out of the canal-like streets
> Weeping arises,
> The weeping of fearing women
> Through all the centuries down."

Surely she was a picture of misery, this woman who was the mother of five fatherless children, forsaken by all, and now earning her livelihood for herself and her children in posing as a model.

Our friend — who had no judgment where suffering was concerned, who suffered with those who suffered, and tried to relieve them as best he could; who could

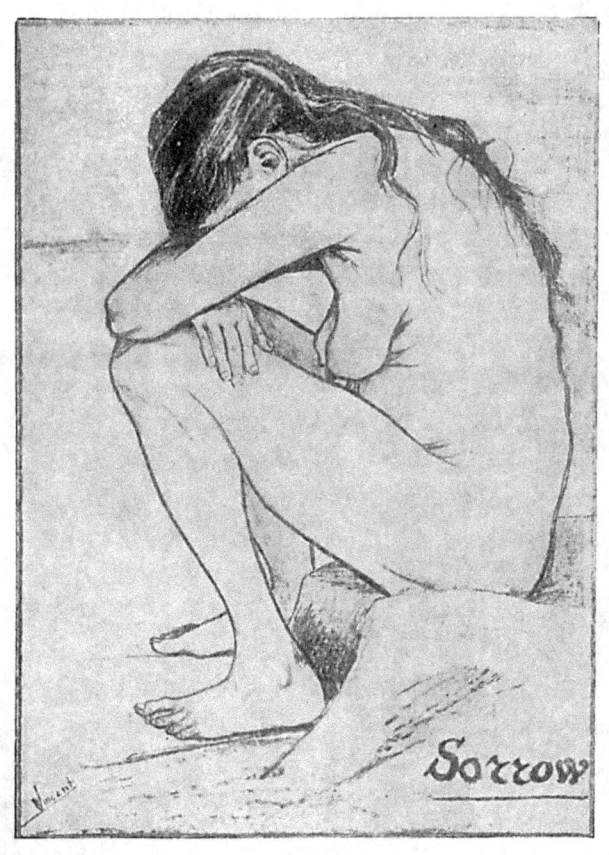

SORROW

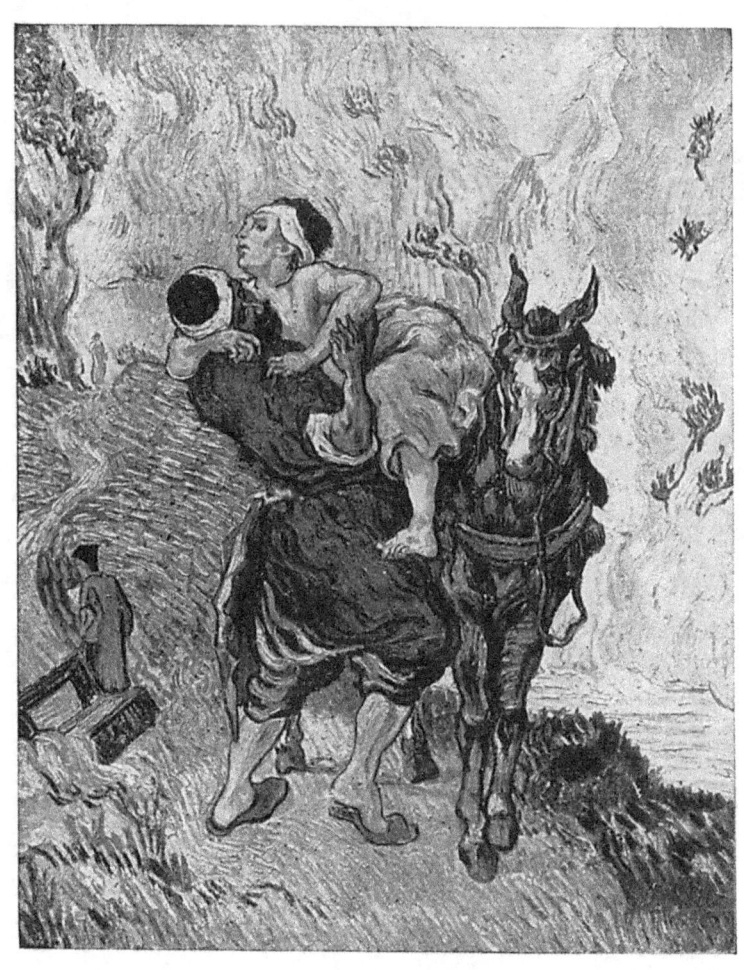

THE GOOD SAMARITAN

never realize that he really had nothing to give, for everything that he could give in the way of clothing or money belonged to another,—offered a roof to this woman and her children. She had told him her tale of misery, the old, old story of the fall, with or without blame, as one wishes to take it, without ever being able to regain her footing; how she was helpless before her fate; how she did not know where to turn; how she had nothing to eat, and no medicine for the little ones when they were ill, and always, always alone — alone with her sorrow. The painter expressed in this picture her story of shame and repentance. The head, with the thin, straight hair, bent low over her spare knees. Sorrow!

The money which was meant for food and lodging, for material and study, naturally could not meet the needs of this helpless family. But who would have thought of trying to keep seven with what was meant for one?

After a while the father, hearing of all this, came personally to see how the matter stood. The landlord had already decided to eject him for nonpayment of rent, and the taxes also were overdue.

Half-starved, he consented, as he did at the Borinage, to return home with his father, who always knew how to care for him most tenderly, as he had keen sympathy for the strangeness of this son. Had he treated him otherwise, what would have become of him or his art?

The woman refused all further offers of help. She

preferred the Bohemian life as a model, and desired to earn her living for herself and her children in the old way.

The place where our painter followed his father was in another part of Brabant, a weavers' section, full of strange poetry; the houses lower, the farms broader than in the other section; the people friendly, plain, workers, farmers, gardeners, and weavers, the last known by their pale, unhealthy faces, since weaving is a harmful trade. In their quiet way they are accustomed to pay most attention to the colors, and to listen to the tick-tack of their looms. Hard-beaten clay is the flooring on which the loom stands. Seldom does one now find the old looms with the carving and the dates of past centuries, where the old oak has blackened, as in the choir stalls of a cathedral. Through a narrow side window the light falls into the low room, with the smoked beams and the dark loom, on the dirty gray figure of the weaver and his white, nervous, never-resting fingers. If one wanders through the village, under the avenue of nut trees, with their heavy foliage, one understands how it was that the peasant poet Burns was aroused to song by the rhythmic tick-tack of the looms.

Sunday evening, shortly before vespers, one could see the weaver, with his sack containing the week's spinning upon his back, wending his way to the modern-built house and shop of the merchant, where was

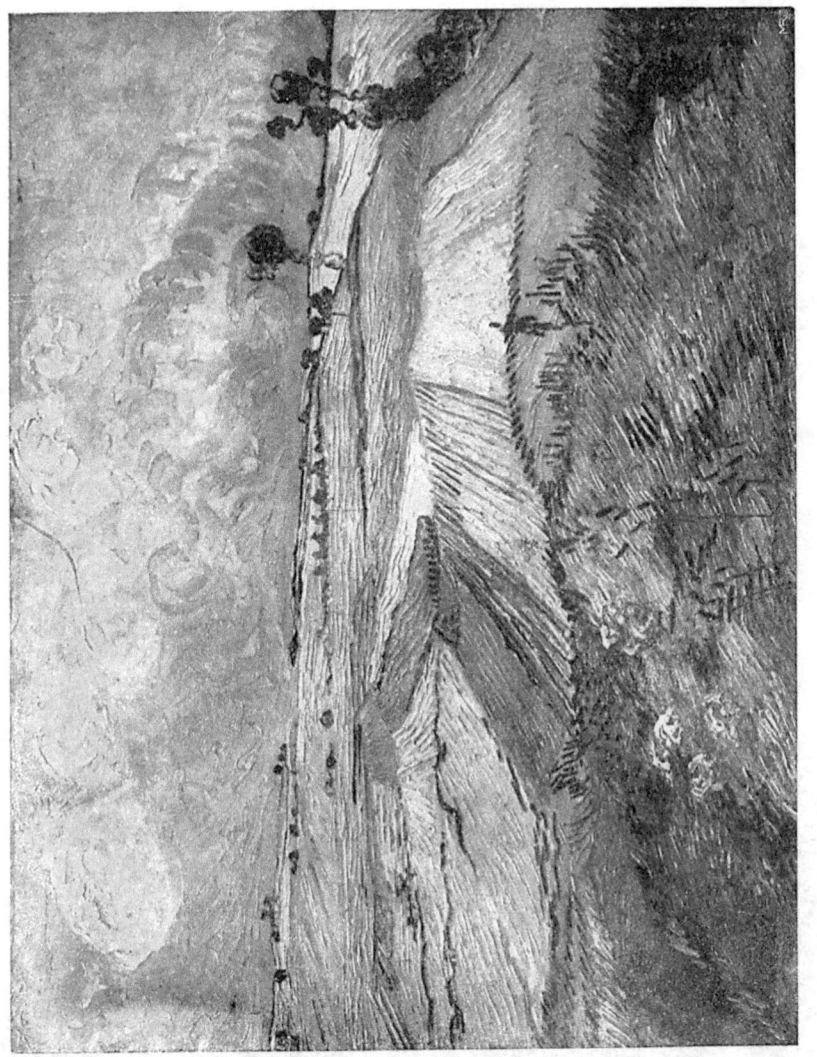

FIELDS NEAR ARLES

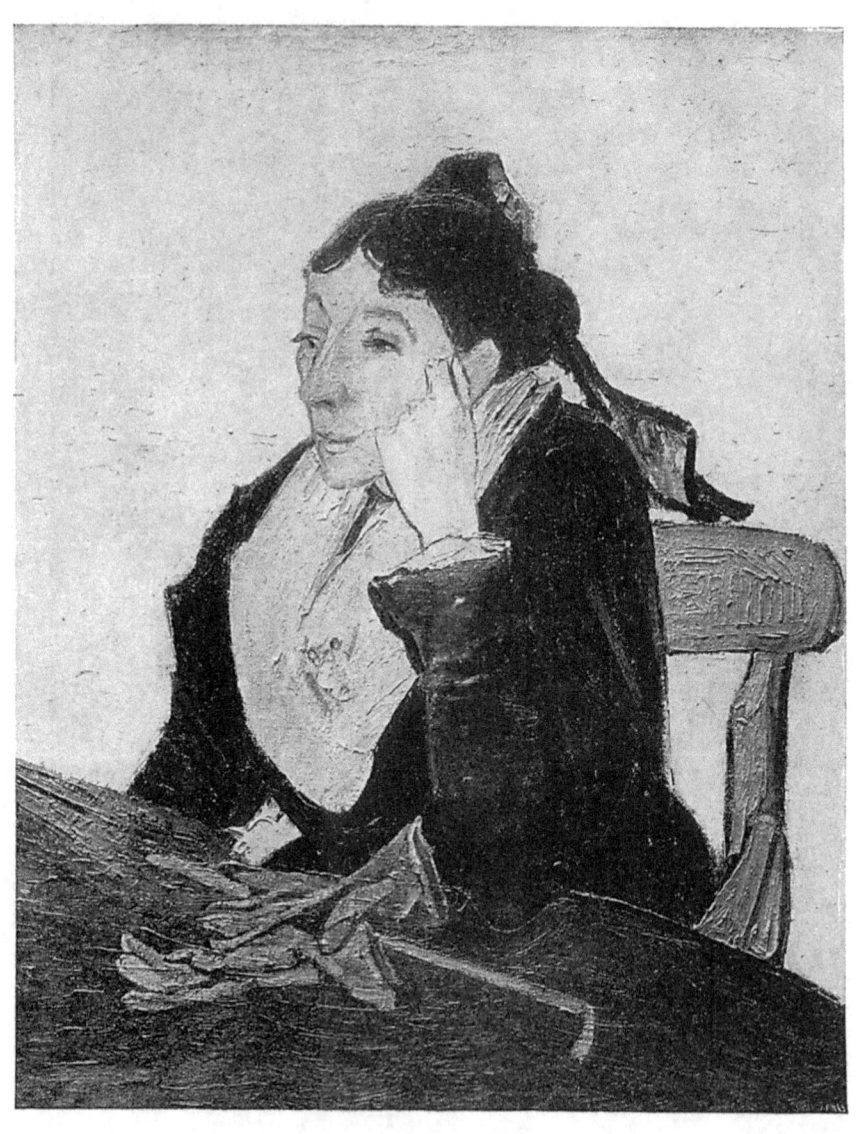

A WOMAN OF ARLES

measured the linen, which is chiefly used by the royal household; and where another sack carefully weighed, containing the threads of the coming week's work, is given in exchange.

Lonely, dreamy figures; alone, or in pairs; seldom in groups; one sees them going along the bare fields in winter where the short green winter corn stands, or in summer, through the waving cornfields, their slow step homesick for the long-looked-for Sunday rest.

For an artist, this was indeed a large field of work. Early in the morning one could see the painter busy at the well behind his parents' cottage, placing his canvas on a stretcher, which a neighboring carpenter had made for him quickly and at small cost; spraying his canvas, or his finished black-and-white drawings, to prevent them from rubbing. Masterly were these charcoal and crayon drawings, which Vincent himself loved to praise. It seemed to him as if during this period he lived his life threefold. An hour meant to him as much as three, according to his achievements. He was indifferent to the distance, or to what he had to carry, if only he could reach his goal. He sought his work where he was sure to find it. No one denied him; all doors were open to him when he wished to paint an interior.

Indifferent to convention or form, a stranger to custom, so that one felt a stranger to him, he was yet beloved by the poor and simple people and those whom Nature had ill-treated. Towards them he showed a simplicity which took away all semblance of presumption. He paid his models well; according to the custom of painters, per hour; and if a child in a high chair sat for him, or an old man in a chimney-corner, he never left without a sweet or an apple for the one, or tobacco for the other, wherewith to while away the time.

Indifferent to appearance, dressed in a blue blouse, the garb of the Flemish peasant, with hair cropped close, a straggly, red-brown beard, eyes ofttimes inflamed from staring at objects in the sun, one would never have taken him to be older than his brothers and sisters, with whom he seldom came in contact. This was not because of any antipathy on either side, but rather the result of their various ways of life. He shared the family meals in a strange fashion. Seated in a corner of the room, his plate on his knee, he would be absorbed in studying a newly painted canvas which stood facing him on a chair. With one hand he would shade his half-closed eyes, while eating with the other. He cut his own bread in thick, heavy slices, which since a child he had preferred eating dry. He also preferred to pour out his own tea or coffee. Deep in his work, he was hardly conscious of what he ate; conscious only of the absorbing problem of how to contrast one color with another or how to balance them. In my opinion in his color lies the great secret of the strong individuality of his art.

Did the name of some writer penetrate through this concentration, he would instantly become alert and take part in the conversation, telling how this or that work had been born because of such and such a personal experience.

He would also compare living authors with the great masters of the past, and would often quote the well-known passage, "All people and all human experiences are at all times the same." His favorite writings were those of Dickens, Carlyle, Beecher-Stowe, Jan Van Beers, Thomas à Kempis, and Solomon's Proverbs.

His listeners were only too ready to give him the floor, he who knew so well of what he was talking. And yet his strangeness always remained a sorrow to his parents. Had he been as others, he would never have had that strange big quality in his work which he has left behind.

Art was his first and only love. Friends, in the real sense of the word, he hardly possessed. His relationship with Van Rappard came nearest to it. They had met in Antwerp; though Van Rappard continued his studies longer, he occasionally visited Vincent in his home.

Van Rappard was a great admirer of his at a time when no one else was. He spoke even then of him as a "tremendous colorist." In the choice of subjects they were singularly alike in taste: groups of wornout workmen in low, ill-ventilated rooms, in which, through a side window, the light streamed; or a picture showing how the hard lot of the workers was lightened through some unexpected happiness. Similar subjects are met with in both their works. Together they painted in Brabant, and during Vincent's stay at The Hague, they spent some time working together at Drente.

While our friend spread his wings to conquer new worlds, Van Rappard remained in the conventional form of the art of his day.

With the exception of this friendship, Vincent had none. In spite of his admiration for the works of Scheffer, Mauve, and others, his inner life they never shared. Unswervingly sure were his steps along the path he had chosen, as Christian on his journey to the Heavenly City.

In the dwelling of the verger of the Catholic church he had his studio, a large, spacious room, which had formerly served as a prayer and knitting school. Several canvases stood against the wall, as he always was working at more than one at the same time. Charcoal drawings were put up; also a number of figure-studies taken from the series he had done in The Hague, and enriched with added figures of his own. Among others, the drawing of the woman with the inscription "Sorrow."

In a corner of the studio stood an old tree, which had been felled by the storm. It had been cut down and placed in a box filled with earth. The crown carried a collection of birds' nests, which Vincent, in his jaunts through the woods, had gathered after the birds had left. There hung the cone-shaped nest of the *Zaumkoenig*, the moss nest of the *faik*, the simple housing of the sparrow, star, and *Krammetsvogel*, and a nest belonging to the nightingale, which showed less skill than the others; also the snow-white, woolly nest of the

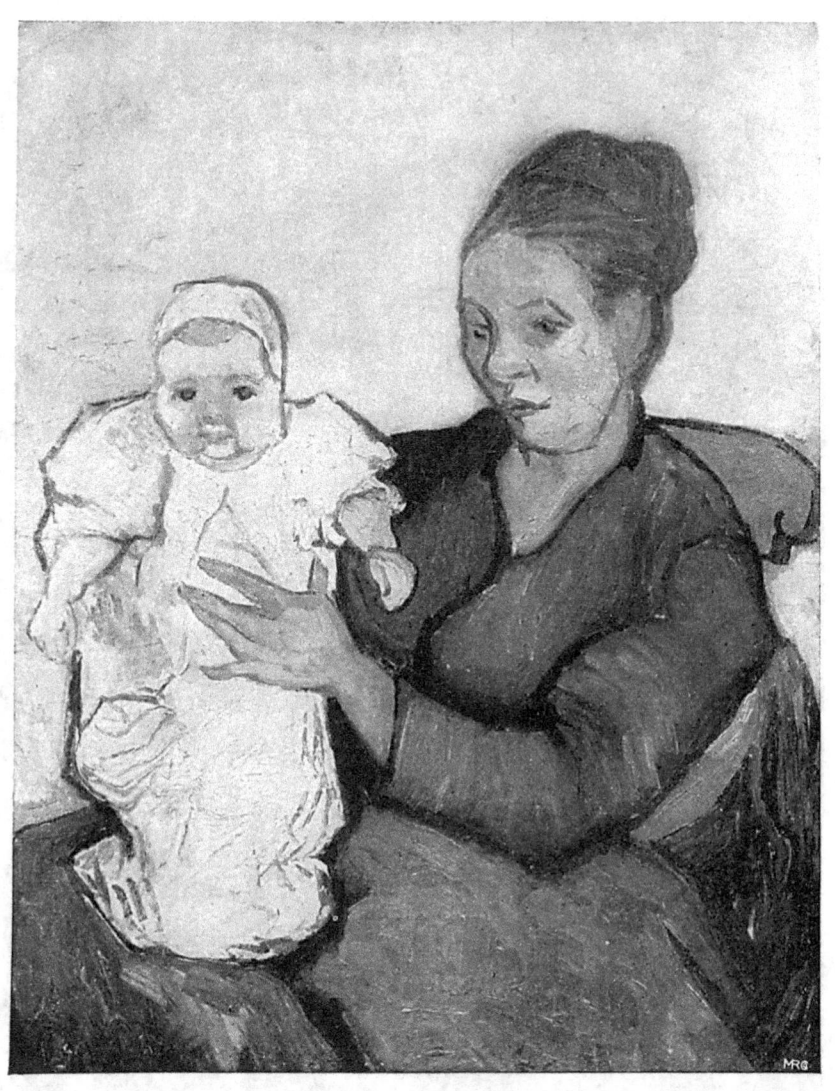

MOTHER AND CHILD

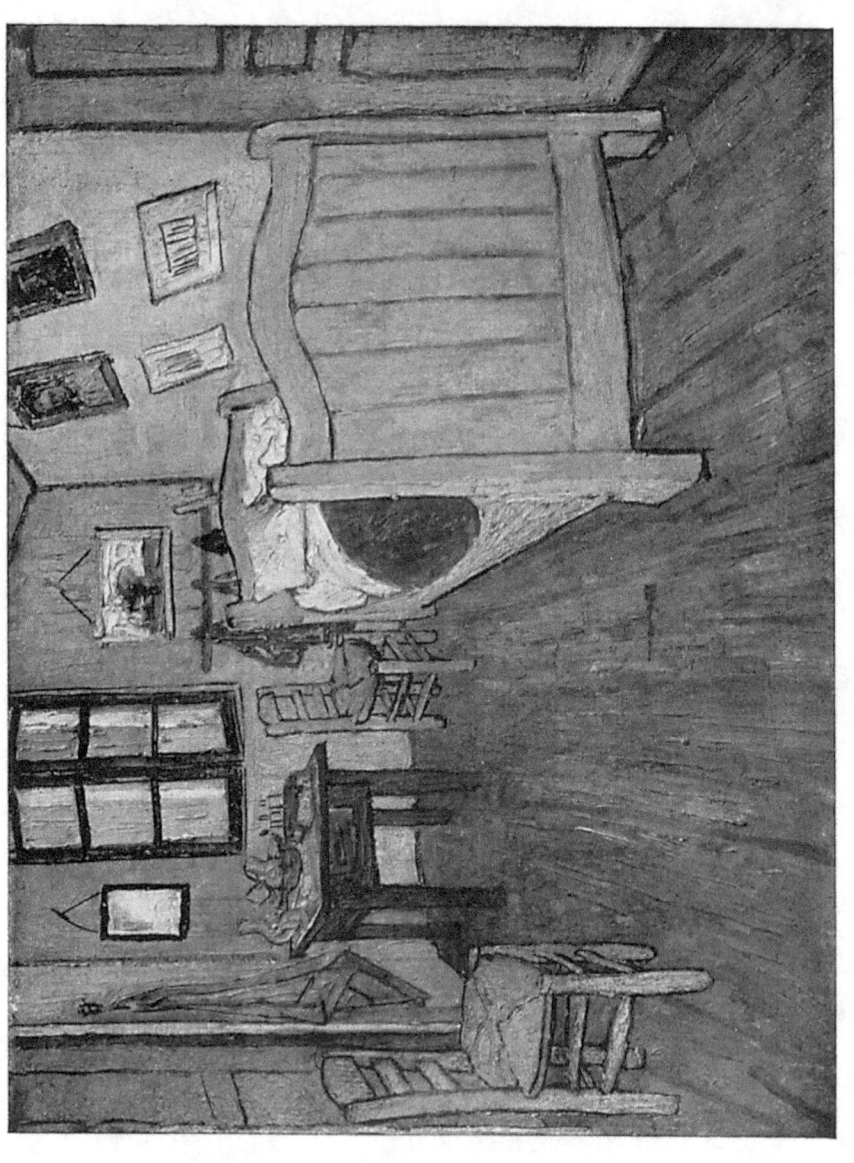

VAN GOGH'S BEDROOM IN ARLES

Wiel Waal, braided out of reeds and lined with soft white down feathers; while in the fork of the tree was the strange little nest of the stream swallow, made out of grass with a flooring of clay; and last of all a pair of nests of those who build low on the ground. He wanted much the nest of the small Bartsch Fisher, which is chiefly made of fish-bones, but it was almost impossible to find one, although he and his younger brother, a school-boy, equally interested in the collection, tried hard to secure one. The collection was a great bond between them. He was far more interested in hearing his brother tell about the life and habits of the birds, and wandering through the woods in search of such trophies, than in his studies.

A curious incident happened one Sunday in February. A heavy forest fire was raging among the pines that stretched along for miles skirting the railroad. A spark from a passing engine had started the fire, and the trees, made unusually dry through a prolonged north gale, burnt like tinder. After the worst of the fire had been conquered, the brothers met most unexpectedly among the smouldering pines. Coming from opposite directions, they had run through the woods and met. Neither could tell why the desire had overcome him, but there they were; the practical, healthy boy, a coming engineer, who seldom read, who only studied because he had to, who was even too lazy to work with his hands, and the painter, untiring, who never was idle, who was absorbed by great problems of color and of art, who was single-minded in his devotion to it,

— here they met, both filled with the one desire to run through the burning forest.

In early spring, when the February fog lingers over the trees and roofs, making them hardly discernible, lending a charm to the entire landscape, wood auctions are held throughout the villages of Brabant, which often lend themselves as entrancing subjects for a picture: wood gathered into piles of loose bundles, enticing to the eyes of the baker; rounded beech blocks, with the light and dark yellow circles at the plane, and stacks of uneven oak. The peasants, running back and forth in their blue blouses and white scrubbed wooden shoes, stand forth clearly from the gray brown of the village streets containing these woodpiles, and the bare trees rising up so straight along the edge of the common.

Something of this kind met Vincent's eyes early one morning. Horrors! He had no colors; they had all been used, and the new lot had not yet arrived. One minute for consideration — then, quickly taking some water-color paper, and gathering from his mother's kitchen some bluing and coffee grounds, he set forth. Eleven o'clock saw him with his sketch complete, containing all the colors the subject offered, the blue and brown, the many varied neutral tints. In spite of the limited material he had mastered his subject; the impression of the foggy village street was there with the woodpiles and the wrangling farmers; everything was rendered in a masterly fashion.

In spite of the beauty of the landscape of Brabant, he

soon felt that she could hold him no longer. His eyes longed for the glowing colors, for the sea of flowers of the South — flowers of all varieties, growing between gorgeous weeds that vied with each other.

His thoughts often carried him back to Paris, for he felt that his eyes had missed much of her beauty at the time he was there. To be able to return to her, to work and to paint, — for that he longed. How much had become clear to his vision since that visit! He had to break with his old technique to reach the brilliancy of color at which he now aimed. From now on one differentiates between his Dutch and French periods.

The sudden death of the father, who had been suffering from heart disease without any one's knowledge, caused the younger brother to return from Paris. The devotion, as well as admiration, which he gave his older brother went hand in hand with the latter's development in his art. Though no artist, Theodor yet possessed the sensibilities of one, which is more than the superficial commonplaces of many a so-called artist who produces pictures. He valued his brother at his real worth. Never for one moment did he doubt the future of Vincent's art.

In spite of the short time that Theodor had held the position for which his brother had shown so little taste, he was called in for consultation, because of his tact, when an important sale was to be made, or to act as guide to well-known people when they desired to see the museums. Notwithstanding his great modesty, he was able to give valuable information with regard to a painter or a picture, and to help his visitor to a better discernment. He was too honest towards his ideals in art not to feel hurt at the moodiness of Fashion, as well as the bad taste she often displayed, honoring the commonplace and pretentious, instead of the beautiful. However, he knew how to handle those with whom he had to deal, and to awaken within them a desire for the best in such a manner that they always thought it was their own choice, and had recognized it of their own accord. "What can I do," he wrote in despair to his sister, who had his complete confidence, "when some one demands a picture, as happened the other day, where the sun and moon must appear simultaneously? I let it be painted, for the taste of such people has sunk too low."

Another time he wrote enthusiastically of an old gentleman from Provence, who had come to Paris to complete the collection in his gallery. Theodor was chosen to assist him. He had learned much through this meeting, and the old gentleman had been kindness itself.

No wonder that the admiration he honestly felt for Vincent's work aroused in him a desire to have others see and admire it. But it was impossible, especially at this time; for though the younger brother received all that the older one produced, he could not succeed in selling one of them — not even the best. Goupil had scorned them, and his was the last word to be said in the Art World of Paris. The only thing left to do was to exchange them for the works of other painters. That was

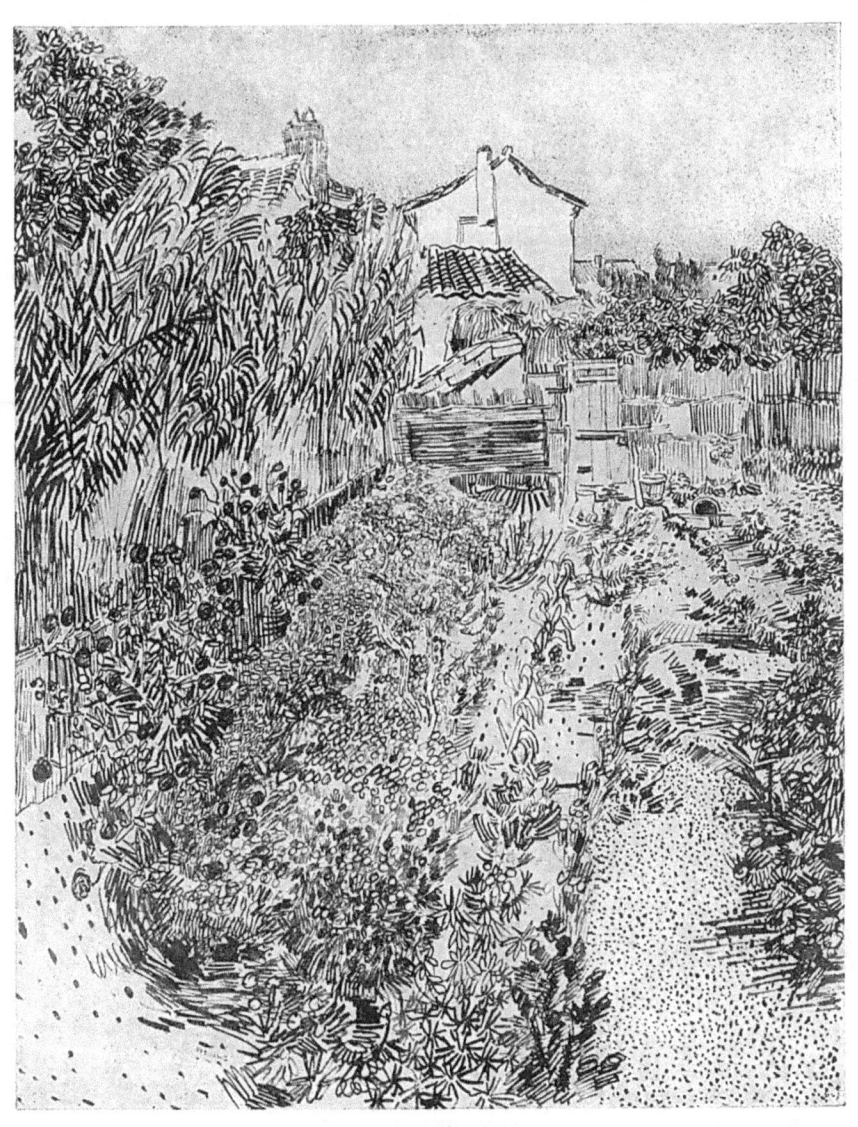

THE GARDEN

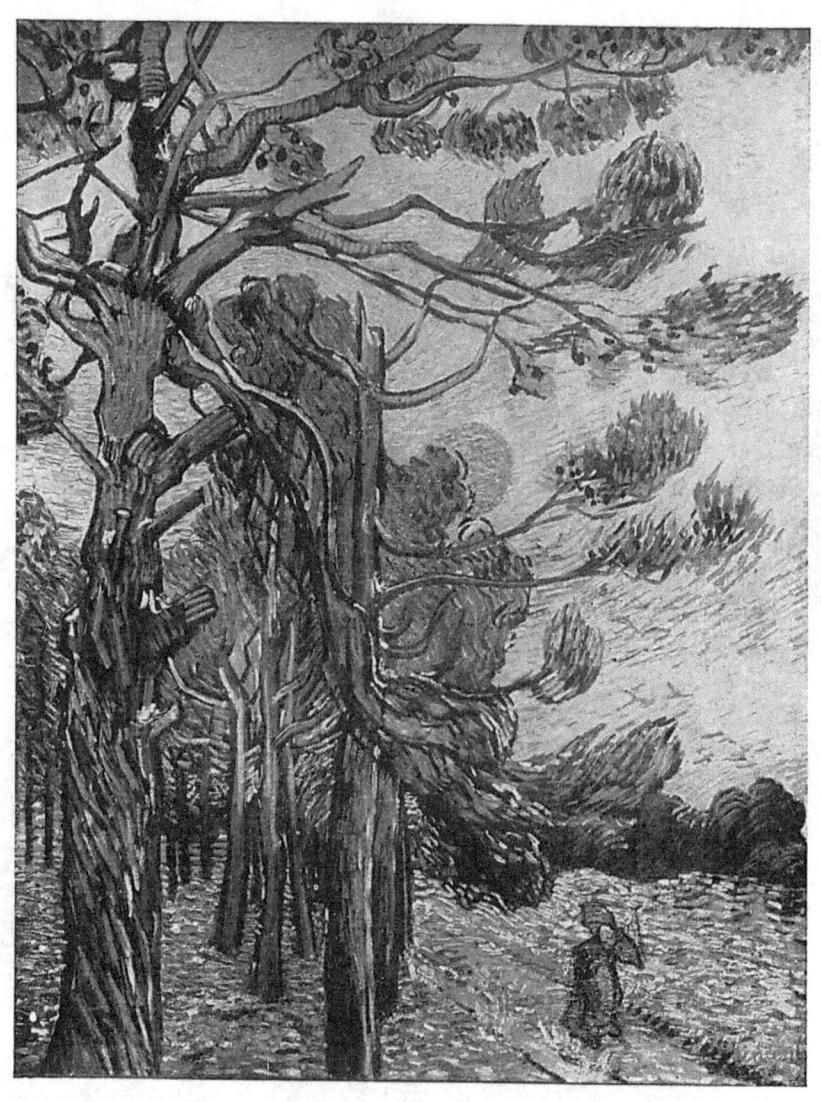

THE PINE TREES

an exchange commission which the artists had among themselves, but after all it only meant a small portion of the pictures. The largest number had to bide their time. It was a great disappointment and sorrow for the younger brother, who always worked for the older one. Besides he knew only too well what it meant to live on a small income, for he had taken his father's burden upon his own shoulders, and now, after his death, met all of Vincent's expenses for further study. On his return he took him to Paris, where they both were lost to Art.

Shakespeare says, "The best poems are those which are never written." The same can be said about pictures, which are often better seen than many a painter can paint. As regards art, the two brothers were one. Both admired the masters of The Hague, — Mauve, Maris, Israels, Mesdag, and also others in certain of their works, but especially dear to their hearts was the French school—Corot, and the fine lyric painter, Millet. " Est ce qu'il n'y a pas une communauté de nature entre tous les vivants de ce monde," Taine says in his "English Literature."

Free as he was from following any one, true as he was to himself alone, yet the spirit of Millet left a strong impression upon him. One can see it in his "Aardappeleeters" in Brabant: the same religious spirit which one finds in the "Angelus" of Millet, and in his "Sower." The former of these is of a man and a woman, who on their return from work bend their heads in reverence at the ringing of the vesper bells.

"It is easier for me to die than to live. Dying is hard, but living still harder," were the words Vincent had said at the death-bed of his father. Hard had been these months before the sudden death of the parent. He had worked unceasingly. The overtaxing of his strength made him sleepless, and one could hear him for hours walking up and down before he found his much-needed rest.

He had to relinquish his studio, for the room was wanted for other purposes. An old laundry in the cellar of his home was put at his disposal, which barely met his needs. The family life, in which he never took part, but with which he came in greater contact since the change, depressed him. Differences of opinion caused him at times to make caustic remarks, which were accepted very differently by various members of his family.

Everywhere there were things to disturb him, to agitate him. Irritation, especially, was shown in a drawing he made at this time, which shows the rear of the family dwelling, with the flower garden. Instead of the old-fashioned house, with the adjoining building sagging a little to one side, and the well-cared-for garden, he made a goblinlike place standing in the midst of wild grass, a few trees bent to one side, furiously whipped by the wind. Some figures also are seen; one cannot tell what they are, or what they do. Masterly is the drawing, very fine in its black and white, as a lithograph: the whole atmosphere ghostlike and eerie. His own spirit of unrest and driven haste forces itself upon one, filling one with evil foreboding.

CHAPTER III

VINCENT went away, and no one saw him again — his mother, nor his sisters, nor his younger brother, who was still a boy.

I am told that letters will be published shortly; they will be like voices from the grave, and may reveal more than these pages, with their meager memories. But those few memories are so dear; they have left so deep a mark on the author, that she needs only to write them down, with gladness in her heart for the sake of truth.

The letters will speak especially of the life in the South.

After staying awhile with his brother in Paris Vincent began to long for the land of colors and song — for Provence. There the colors would be aglow and would be imprisoned by him upon the canvas; as in the flower of our old Dutch school a few knew how to imprison both flowers and fruit.

Now and then he would send a picture to Holland, to keep his family in touch with his work. The letters Theodor wrote home sounded more and more hopeful, for he, being more connoisseur than dealer, read future fame in the works of his brother, who was the object of all his concern, his love, his never-ending devotion and sympathy.

Always did one have to care for Vincent, who was

totally blind to everyday needs, who had to be spared
all strain if he was to accomplish that which he had
set himself to do. His father had cared for him with
never-ending tenderness, and this same care his brother
now gave him. Theodor was married, and later father
of a son who bore the name of Vincent, but his brother
always held the same place in his heart.

Vincent's works were continually declared unsalable.
The temptation to turn his back on the commercial art
world, as Vincent desired, Theodor withstood. His was
too practical a nature. One advance was made, however. A small art dealer, whose shop was only the width
of a window, who was friend and protector, as far as
was in his power, of many a poor, nameless beginner,
offered to exhibit at least one picture every now and
then. But to show Vincent's work without causing a
stir, that was impossible.

So it came to pass that his pictures began to be seen
and reviewed — that at least was a beginning. But
the glimmering fire of his genius, that showed itself
outwardly in its burst of color, was devouring him
inwardly and undermining his physical condition.
Through untiring work his nervous system became unstrung, especially the overwrought sight. Painting in
the blinding sun, and at twilight, were more than his
eyes could stand.

Now and then epileptic attacks would show themselves. Long before their appearance, they would torment him through difficulty in breathing, an oppres-
sion which is described in a letter and which demanded

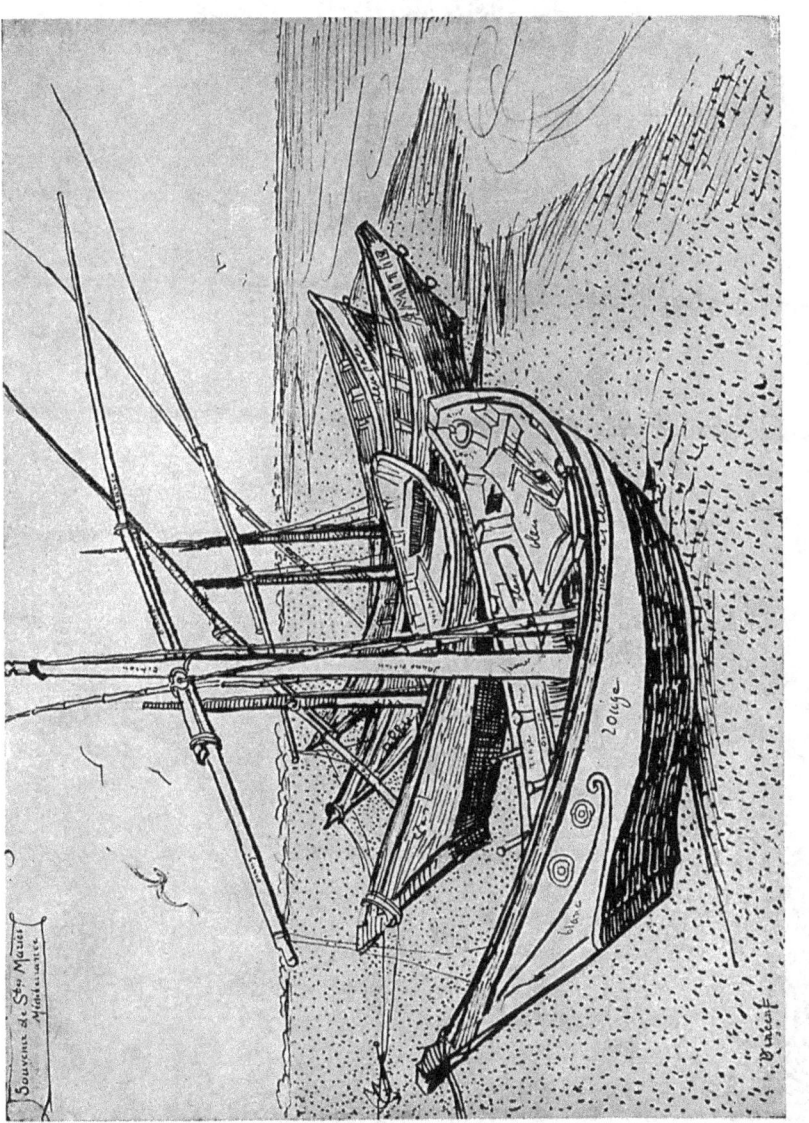

SKETCH AT LES SAINTES MARIES

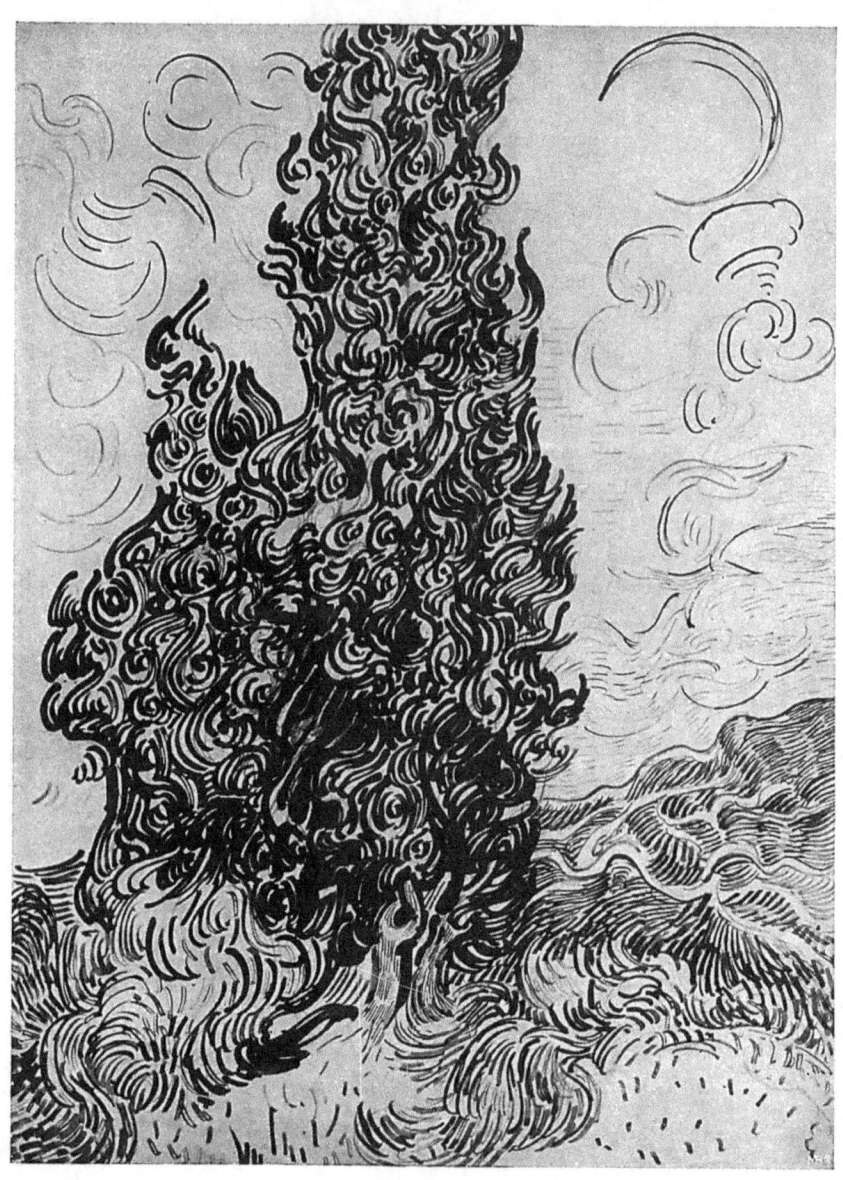

THE CYPRESSES

weeks of enforced rest. What must such enforced rest
not have meant to a spirit of his activity!

These physical disturbances brought with them at
times a mental depression which nothing could dispel.
And the terrible part was that these attacks increased
rather than diminished. Again and again he had to go
to the hospital at Arles for treatment. While there he
painted a beautiful picture — the rear and garden of
the hospital. Now that I mention it, I wish I might have
it before me, as many another, which are constantly being exhibited in various European cities. Among them is
surely the "Provence Herdsman," and another known
as "La Berceuse."

While he was lying in the ward of the hospital after
one of his sad attacks, an old man of strange appearance was brought to the neighboring section. His exterior reminded the painter of a picture of one of the pa-
triarchal fathers, as painted by an old Flemish master.
Over eighty was this old herdsman, who had tended
his flock since childhood, along the southern plains. He
had always lived in the open without a hut, and his
covering had been the skin of some wild animal. His
bed had been the flowering heather, his food the milk
from his herd and some dried fruits, which the village
folk sometimes brought to him and which had to last
a good while. His life had run its course. Hardly dis-
tinguishable were the years, as one season followed another, as a day silently steals into dusk, which loses
itself again in night; a life of even tenor — clear as a
starlit night, "pur comme un ciel étoilé."

Overcome by a frost of unusual severity for that section of the country, he was found stiff — half dead, one
morning. One thought one saw signs of life, and the
people who came from the town to carry the milk back
from the meadows took the old man to Arles, where he
was taken to the hospital to be revived. The doctors
feared it was only a question of hours, since the frost
had attacked the region of the heart. When he revived,
he told them the story of his life, and was grateful for
the good bed and shelter which should have been his
long ago. No wonder that his face left so deep an impression upon the painter that he was forced to trans-
fer it to canvas.

The counter-piece to this picture is "La Berceuse."
It is the picture of a woman who lives in the ancient
folklore of the Provence sailors, who hums to the fisherman the old songs his mother sang at his cradle, when
the storm grows too mighty for his boat, and death
beckons relentlessly from the sea. Then the fisherman
hears from the lips of La Berceuse the cradle-songs of
long ago — so the legend runs.

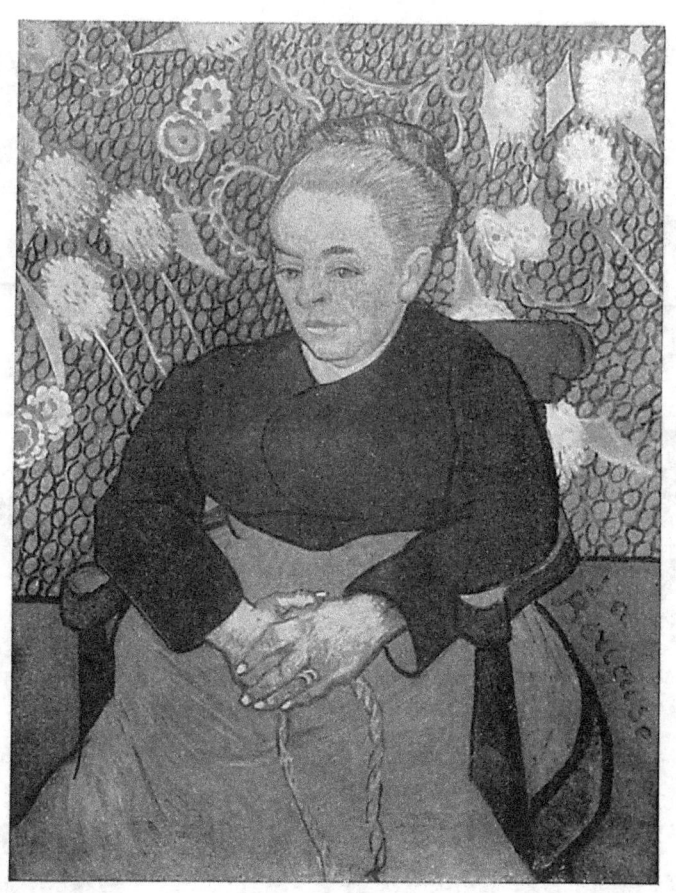

LA BERCEUSE

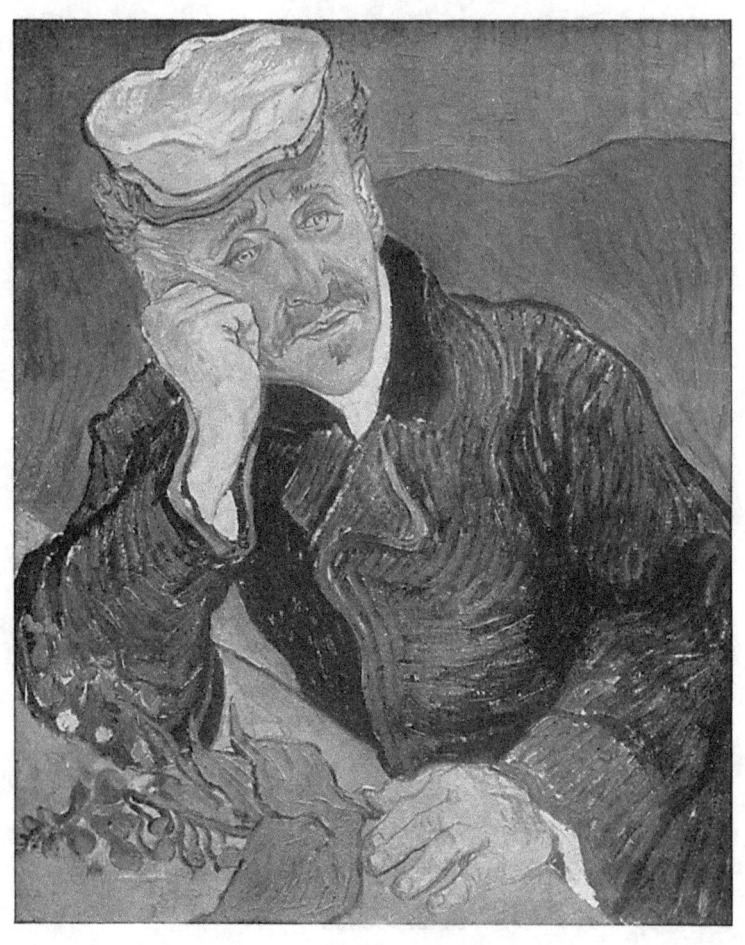

DR. GACHET

CHAPTER IV

THE END

THE continued recurrence of Vincent's ill-health filled the younger brother with alarm.' What would be the end of all these terrible attacks? His fears were not unfounded. Once already had he been called to the South in great haste, and had discovered his brother in such a critical condition at the hospital that showed his fears were not without cause. How hard was the uncertainty for him who could so ill be spared from the office, and who never knew when these depressions would conquer his brother; he, who cared for him with a tenderness a mother gives her sick child. "Greater love hath no man than to give his life for his brother." Such was the love he gave Vincent.

He decided to arrange, if possible, to have him nearer Paris. In a small village on the Saône he knew of a physician, a man more artist than doctor, under whose care his brother should be placed. As far as his large practice permitted him, he was to keep an eye on the artist when these sad attacks showed their first symptoms.

As Vincent's father had known when to suggest new plans, so his brother knew, too, and chose his opportunity, when the artist was feeling weak and ill, to persuade him to follow him to this new place. It was a lovely spot, this last home he was to know, and he arrived with the spring.

Its beauty was less brilliant than in the South, but Nature appeared at the height of her entrancing charm. A rolling country, full of flowering gardens, interspersed with woodland; a cottage overgrown with roses; here and there a Roman tower, or an old wall, an old abbey or church built of sandstone; such was the lovely peaceful French landscape.

Once more he was filled with a desire to work and to paint. He took mahlstick, palette, and a bundle of brushes and began work. Before the first picture was finished, he started a second, a third, in his studio.

To the places he had found while tramping in search for subjects he now took his easel, and began working under the blazing sun. He produced as the summer did in all its lavishness. In this land of flowers, his flower studies reached their full height, and he painted his sunflowers.

"Darest thou now, O soul,
  Walk out with me toward the unknown region
  Where neither ground is for the feet nor any path to follow?

"Then we burst forth, we float,
  In Time and Space, O soul, prepared for them,
  Equal, equipt at last, O joy, O fruit of all them to fulfil, O
    soul!"[1]

Science had foretold it. The old trouble forced its
return. Following upon the strain of work, faintness,
that horror of all painters, threatened him. To him
spasms, fear, and despair were one and the same —
a despair which caused him to fear life more than
death.

His brother was on his way to join his young family, consisting of wife and child, in Holland, where they
had gone to spend the summer vacation. Fortunately,
some work had detained him a week longer in Paris.
A telegram from his friend the doctor advised his im-
mediate coming to Auvers. He instinctively felt the
condition in which he would find his brother. Mechan-
ically he ordered his affairs and hurried to the station,
throwing himself into the next train, where he spent
the few hours of the journey half paralyzed by fear. He
arrived in time. As if to reward him for all his love, his
tender care, his self-sacrifice, it was given him to close
the eyes of him he had loved so intensely, as one can

---

[1] Walt Whitman.

only love one for whom the whole heart hungers, where every breath, heartbeat, and thought is not for self, but for the other.

His brother was still living when he arrived. The morning of the same day Vincent had left the house, as was his wont, carrying with him all that he thought he needed for his work. It was a scorching day in July. His innkeeper, who knew of his illness, became worried when towards three he had not come back, for he generally returned for dinner, bringing one canvas, to set out with another, according to the hour and light of the day. They found him senseless, but living, and carried him home. Dying was easier for him than living, and he went halfway to meet the Great Reaper — Death.

The doctor came and, himself deeply affected, did all that could be done, telegraphed his brother and remained at the bedside.

A letter out of the past, worn and yellow with age, which Theodor Van Gogh wrote his sister, will speak with his own voice above the quiet of the grave: —

". . . They say it is well that he is at rest. I hesitate to say so. I feel rather it is one of the cruelest tragedies of life. He is to be counted among the martyrs who died smiling. . . .

"He had no desire to live, and he was content, because he had fought unflinchingly for his conviction, which he had tested with the best and noblest who had gone before him. A test is his love for his father, his

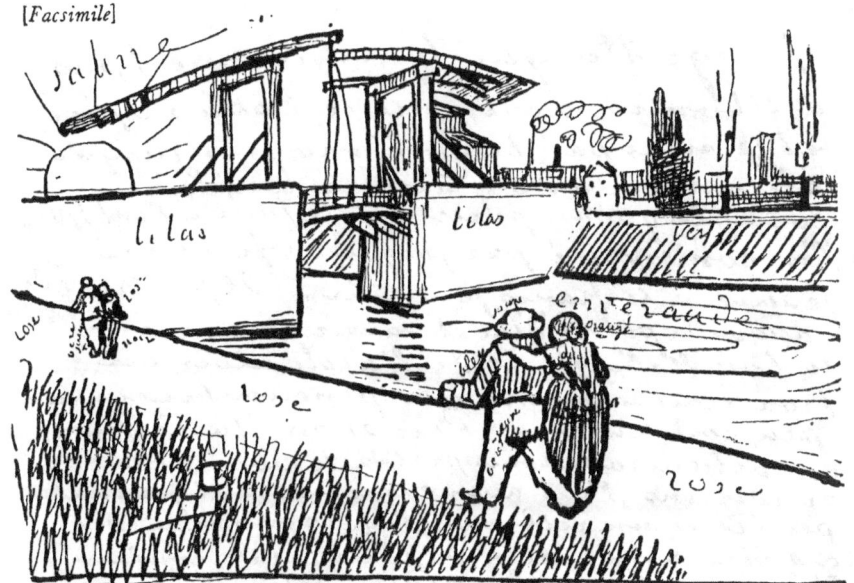

Mon cher Bernard, ayant promis de
t'écrire, je veux commencer par te
dire que le pays me paraît aussi
beau que le Japon pour la limpidité
de l'atmosphère et les effets de couleur
gaie. Les eaux font des tâches d'un
bel émeraude et d'un riche bleu dans les
paysages ainsi que nous le voyons
dans les crepons. Des couchers de soleil
orange pâle faisant paraître bleu les
terrains. Des soleils jaunes splendid.
Cependant je n'ai encore guère vu le
pays dans sa splendeur habituelle d'été.
Le costume des femmes est joli, et le dimanche
surtout on voit sur le boulevard des
arrangements de couleur très naïfs et
bien trouvés. Et cela aussi sans doute
s'égayera encore en été

Je regrette que la vie ici n'est pas
à si bon marché que je l'avais espéré
et je n'ai pas trouvé moyen jusqu'à
présent de m'en tirer à aussi bon
compte qu'on pourrait le faire à Pont Aven
J'ai commencé par payer 5 fr et maintenant
je suis à 4 francs par jour. Il faudrait
savoir le patois d'ici et savoir manger de
la bouillabaisse et de l'aioli alors on
trouverait sûrement une pension bourgeoise
peu coûteuse. Puis si on était à plusieurs
on obtiendrait, je suis porté à le croire, des
conditions plus avantageuses. Il y aurait
peut être un réel avantage pour bien des
artistes amoureux de soleil et de couleur
s'émigrer dans le midi. Si les Japonais
ne sont pas en progrès dans leur pays
il est indubitable que leur art se continue
en France. En tête de cette lettre je
t'envoie un petit croquis d'une étude
qui me préoccupe pour en faire quelque
chose. Des matelots qui remontent avec
leurs amoureuses vers la ville qui profile
l'étrange silhouette de son pont levis sur
un énorme soleil jaune
J'ai une autre étude du même
pont levis avec un groupe de
laveuses. Serai content d'un
mot de toi pour savoir ce que
tu fais et où tu iras. Poignée
de main bien cordiale à
toi même et aux amis b. à t.
                                    Vincent

love for the Gospel, for the poor and miserable, for the Masters in literature and art. In his last letter, dated four days before his death, he writes: 'I try just as hard as certain other painters do, whom I have loved and honored.'

"One must acknowledge that he was a great artist; to be a great man often goes hand in hand. Time will bring the honor due him, and many a one will grieve to think he died so young. He himself desired to die. While I was sitting by him, trying to persuade him that we would heal him, and that we hoped he would be saved from further attacks, he answered: 'La tristesse durerat toujours.' I felt I understood what he wished to say.

"Shortly afterward he was seized with another attack, and the next minute closed his eyes.

"The people in that lovely village held him in high esteem. From all sides one heard how beloved he was, and many followed him to the grave. There a stone will speak his name to the passer-by.

"I have decided to organize an exhibition of his works in Paris within the next few months. I wish you could see a collection of his pictures. One has to see them together to understand them truly. I presume they will write about him. If I succeed in getting a room, the exhibition is to be in October, when the Parisians are back in town. . . .

. . . "He will not be forgotten."

August 5, 1890.

How truly has been fulfilled the prophecy with which
the letter. closes! Much has been written, much that
is not true. A placè of honor has been given his pictures
in the museums of the principal cities of the Nether-
lands. Many eyes, abroad as well as at home, that did
not appreciate him during his lifetime, are turned towards his work.

Influenced by an understanding of art, as well as a
commercial spirit, but above all by piety, it has been
the tactful hand of a woman (Frau Cohen-Goschalk,
widow of Theodor Van Gogh) that has broken the
path that has brought recognition for Vincent's work,
and beaten down the high walls of stiff convention,
which in the beginning condemned his art.

Since the day, more than twenty years ago, that the
remains of the artist were carried to their last resting-
place, in that land of color and sunshine, countless
European cities have held exhibitions of his pictures,
which were reviewed in foreign and home papers according to their insight and belief.

Buried in flowers, amongst others his sunflower,
which he loved so well, stood the bier in the middle of
the studio. His brother, attended by a group of artists,
who had come down from Paris for the services, carried him to the grave. There the brother, overcome
with sorrow, lost consciousness. "It was as if the brother called his brother from the grave," wrote Bernard,
painter and writer, friend and admirer of the one, and
friend of the family of the other. Thus he describes in
an article the unutterable sorrow through which the

brother was passing, an article which will surely appear in the volume of letters to be published, which glows with the genius of the one in the recognition of the other.

Concerning these personal recollections, may they be as said the prophet Isaiah: "They will not return empty-handed, but will do that which is pleasing unto me."

It was a long time before I could comprehend Vincent Van Gogh's art, but at last my eyes were opened. That may be the cause of the totally different judgments one heard in the Autumn Exhibition of 1908, where some could not tear themselves away, while others, shrugging their shoulders, declared him insane. Though these judgments differed to such a marked extent, yet must all acknowledge his strength, daring, and boldness of knowledge, shown in the deliberate choice of the balance of color — must acknowledge that his pictures are the work of a man who labored during the heat of the day, until night came, when he could labor no more.

To prove the clearness and simplicity of his vision, to show that the art of description held even pace with his whole development, to prove in what measure he had mastered the French language, this little bit of prose follows, which my brother sent me: —

"Il y a 25 ans environ, qu'un homme de Granville partit pour L'Angleterre. Après la mort de son père ses freres se disputaient l'héritage, et tâchaient sourtout de lui soustraire sa part. Las de se quereller, il leur abandonna sa part et partit pauvre pour Londres, où il obtint une place de maître de Français à une école. Il avait 30 ans lorsqu'il se maria avec une Anglaise bien plus jeune que lui; il eut l'enfant, une fille.

"Apres avoir été marié 7 ou 8 ans, sa maladie de poitrine s'agravit.

"Un de ses amis lui demanda alors s'il avait encore quelque désir, à quoi il répondit, qu'avant de mourir il aimerait à revoir son pays.

"Son ami lui paya les frais du voyage.

"Il partit donc, malade jusqu'a là mort, avec sa femme et sa fille de 6 ans pour Granville. Là il loua une chambre à des pauvres gens demeurant près de la mer.

"Le soir il se faisait porter sur la grêve et regardait le soleil se coucher dans la mer. Un soir, voyant qu'il était près de mourir, les gens avertissent sa femme qu'il était temps s'envoyer chercher le curé pour qu'il donnât l'extrême onction au malade.

"Sa femme qui était protestante s'y opposa, mais il dit, 'Laissez les faire.'

"Le curé arriva donc et le malade se confessa devant tous les gens de la maison.

"Alors tous les assistants ont pleuré en entendant cette vie juste et pure.

"Après il voulut qu'on le laissat seul avec sa femme; quand ils furent seuls il l'embrassa et dit, ' Je t'ai aimée.' Alors il mourut . . .

"Il aimait la France, la Bretagne surtout, et la nature, et il voyait Dieu; c'est à cause de cela que je vous
raconte la vie de cet étranger sur la terre, qui cependant
en fut un des vrais citoyens."

(Signed, Vincent Van Gogh.)

(Almost 25 years ago, a man from Granville journeyed
to England. After the death of his father, his brothers
fought over the inheritance, and especially strove to
keep his share from him. As he wearied of the fight,
he gave them his share and journeyed to London in
poverty, where he found a position as teacher of French
in a school. He was thirty when he married an English
girl, who was much younger than he. He had one
child, a daughter.

After being married seven or eight years, his con-
sumption grew worse. One of his friends asked him if he
had any desire, whereupon he answered, he would like
to see his own country before he died. His friend met
his expenses. He traveled in a dying condition to Granville, accompanied by his wife and little six-year-old
daughter. There he rented a room at the house of some
poor people living by the sea.

In the evening he was wont to be carried to the
shore, where he watched the setting sun. One evening,
the people who noticed how near he was to dying advised the wife that it was time to call a priest to give
him the last sacrament.

His wife, a Protestant, objected, but he said, "Let
it be." The Priest came, and the sick man made his

confession before all the people of the house. All who were present wept when they heard of his pure and righteous life. Thereupon, he asked to be left alone with his wife. When they were alone, he embraced her, and said, "I loved you"; then he died.

He loved France, especially Brittany, and Nature, and he beheld God. That is why I have told you of the life of the "stranger of this world," who, nevertheless, was one of her truest citizens.)

(Signed, Vincent Van Gogh.)